D0982431

COMPETING IN CAPABILITIES

Competing
in
Capabilities

The Globalization Process

JOHN SUTTON

OXFORD
UNIVERSITY PRESS

OXFORD

UNIVERSITY PRESS

Great Clarendon Street, Oxford, OX2 6DP,
United Kingdom

Oxford University Press is a department of the University of Oxford.
It furthers the University's objective of excellence in research, scholarship,
and education by publishing worldwide. Oxford is a registered trade mark of
Oxford University Press in the UK and in certain other countries

Published in the United States of America by Oxford University Press
198 Madison Avenue, New York, NY 10016, United States of America

British Library Cataloguing in Publication Data
Data available

Library of Congress Cataloguing in Publication Data
Data Available

ISBN 978-0-19-927453-6

For Jules, Nick, and Will

Acknowledgments

The origins of this volume began with my Keynes Lecture of 2000 to the British Academy (Sutton 2001) which I developed further as the Clarendon Lectures of 2004. My Presidential Address to the Royal Economic Society, which forms the basis of Chapters 1 and 3 below, and my recent joint paper with Dan Trefler which forms the basis of Chapter 2, allowed me to crystallize and develop some ideas set out in the Lectures.

I would like to thank Ana Valero, Clemens Von Oertzen, Qi Zhang, and the students in my 'Globalization and Strategy' course of 2011–12 for their careful reading of the draft version of this volume.

And one final thank you to all my colleagues in the 'Capabilities' lunch group, for the best conversations I have had on this subject.

Contents

List of Figures

List of Boxes

History and Theory

The globalization process we have witnessed over the past twenty years is just the latest act in a long-term drama. The first great wave of globalization occurred in the latter half of the nineteenth century; the second took off in the years following the Second World War; the current act began with the opening up of China and India and the collapse of the Soviet Union.

All three phases have much in common: the growth of trade volumes, the flow of international capital, and the ramifications that these bring. Yet each act has been distinct in terms of the most salient features of the process – and each has led, in its turn, to a new body of economic analysis concerned with its interpretation. Great events cast a long shadow: history shapes theory.

GLOBALIZATION IN HISTORY

The second half of the nineteenth century witnessed a massive opening up of world markets. The spread of the railways and improvements in shipping led to falling transport costs. Tariff barriers were falling in the industrialized world. Huge flows of capital moved across the globe, while improvements in shipping and the developments of rail networks drastically reduced transport costs, leading to a boom in the trade of commodities and manufactures.

The great drivers of trade in this period, as contemporaries well understood, were 'differences in factor endowments': the land-rich Americas exported agricultural produce to Europe, which in turn exported manufactured goods to the Americas. This process of trade based on comparative advantage between parts of the world in which the ratio of land to labour (or fixed capital stock) differed substantially, was familiar since the days of David Ricardo. Such trade tends to bring about a convergence in factor prices: wage rates in the new world, as compared with the old, would rise as a result of the increased demand for labour driven by the new trade flows.

The codification of the economics underlying this process did not come about until much later. The standard formulation is due to Heckscher and Ohlin, both of whom wrote their key works in the 1920s. Their analysis of the links from factor endowments to commodity and factor prices provided testable predictions of the theory: but data was lacking. Only very recently, in the work of O'Rourke and Williamson (2001), has a wide-ranging and systematic analysis of the predicted 'factor price convergence' been attempted. The results, subject to caveats about limitations imposed by data availability, suggest strongly that the classical Heckscher–Ohlin models capture the primary mechanisms driving the process in this period: it was indeed an era of factor-endowment driven trade.

THE POST SECOND WORLD WAR ERA

The wave of globalization that followed the Second World War began with the establishment of new international institutions (the IMF, the World Bank, and GATT) and the formation of the European Economic Community. It was marked by a major lowering of tariff barriers and a huge increase in the volume of international trade. But what struck many economists at the time as the most remarkable feature of the process was the role of intra-industry trade between very similar industrial economies. In other words, the paradigm case involved the export of German cars to France, and French cars to Germany – the trade was 'within the industry', in contrast to the pattern captured in the Heckscher–Ohlin framework. Differences in factor intensity between France and Germany were extremely small: the driver of this 'intra-industry' trade was clearly different in kind.

The dominance of this 'intra-industry' type of trade within the newly established European Economic Community was demonstrated by Balassa (1967). By the 1970s some models of this type of trade had been proposed Grubel and Lloyd (1975), but it was the publication of

Paul Krugman's article of 1979 that sparked off a new literature based on 'monopolistic competition' models. In these models, competing products offered by different firms were 'horizontally differentiated', i.e. if they were offered at equal prices, some consumers would prefer one variety while others would choose a different variety.[1] The production of any product ('variety') involved both a fixed cost, and a constant marginal cost ('increasing returns'). Under free entry, a number of firms offering different products would be present in the market; their equilibrium prices would exceed marginal cost, and their gross profit margins would suffice to cover their fixed (or sunk) costs.

Now if two economies of this kind are joined via free trade, all consumers gain access to the varieties produced in both countries. This means lower prices, as a larger number of firms come into competition with each other. The new long-run equilibrium number of firms will be less than the total number existing across both countries in the pre-liberalization set-up; each firm will have a higher sales volume, however, so its average cost (including the contribution to fixed costs) will be correspondingly less – and it is this 'exploitation of scale economies' that constitutes both the driver of the trade flows, and the source of welfare gains from trade in this setting.

This, then, was the story economists came to tell about the drivers of trade in the post-war era. As with the Heckscher–Ohlin model, this view took some time to become codified and accepted; it was not until the 1980s that it became the standard way of looking at these issues.

One feature of these 'intra-industry' trade models that cast a long shadow in the trade literature, was their reliance on a 'monopolistic competition' framework. In such a setting, any fixed or sunk costs of entry are exogenous (i.e. their size is determined by technological considerations, outside the control of firms). A central implication of this, is that as the global market gets larger, more and more firms enter each industry, so all industries can become fragmented (i.e. occupied by a large number of firms, each of whom has a very small market share). This is precisely the feature that seems a poor representation of many global industries – such as aircraft, pharmaceutical, or video games – and it is this that will form our point of departure in Chapter 1.

In what follows, we turn to the third of our 'waves of globalization', which began with the opening up of the Chinese and Indian

---

[1] This is in contrast to 'vertical product differentiation', i.e. differentiation by quality. In this latter setting, if two goods whose quality differs are offered at the same price, then all consumers will choose the same ('high-quality') good.

economies, and with the collapse of the Soviet Union. What appears to be the dominant feature of this recent era, is neither 'factor differences' driven trade (though this certainly forms an important element in the story developed below), nor is it 'trade between equals'. Rather, what seems most striking here, is the opening up of trade between parts of the world in which the initial levels of industrial capabilities were widely different. This suggests taking a different point of departure in modelling the process.

THE CURRENT PHASE

The most salient feature of the process we have seen at work over the past twenty years is the transformation of productivity and quality levels, and the widening of the range of products offered on international markets, by China, India, and the economies of Eastern Europe. The roots of this process are various. In some cases, the widened opportunities available to firms in these countries stimulated local firms to respond. More typically, partnerships of one kind or another with foreign firms, or the entry of foreign firms operating plants alone, was the key vehicle. But whatever the mechanism, the outcome was a striking transformation from a population of firms that hugely lagged behind global standards of productivity and quality, to one which could compete effectively in global markets. Central to this story was the role played by 'quality', an element long relegated to the footnotes of International Economics. But over the past decade, a new literature has emerged on 'Quality and Trade', which is deeply concerned with these issues. Meanwhile, economists have begun to build bridges towards their Business School colleagues, who have long grappled with the closely intertwined question of firms' 'capabilities'. It is these lines of analysis that I want to explore in what follows.[2]

---

[2] A large literature on trade and quality has developed in recent years: see for example Feenstra (1984), Schott (2004), Hummels and Klenow (2005), Hallak (2006), Verhoogen (2008), Hallak and Schott (2011), Kugler and Verhoogen (2012), Khandelwal (2010). These authors as well as Hummels and Skiba (2004), Schott (2008), Choi, Hummels, and Xiang (2009), Johnson (2012), and Baldwin and Harrigan (2011) examine the relationship between trade flows and quality. Verhoogen (2008) explores the relationship between quality, trade, and inequality, as do Goldberg and Pavcnik (2007). Amiti and Khandelwal (2009) explore the impact of trade restrictions on quality upgrading. Hallak and Sivadasan (2009) and Bastos and Silva (2010) provide

The novelty of the present treatment, relative to the 'Quality and Trade' literature, is that, by developing a framework that has proved useful in the Industrial Organization literature, the 'Cournot Model with Quality', it builds a bridge from the IO literature both to the Management literature on Capabilities, and to the Trade literature. One key feature of this framework is that it *endogenizes* the notion of scarce (and so valuable) capabilities, showing *why* it must always be the case that some capabilities remain relatively scarce at equilibrium. This idea, central to the 'market structure' literature in Industrial Organization, will be our point of departure in Chapter 1.

Each of the three chapters that follow begins by introducing a single key assumption, and what follows is a working out of its implications. These three key assumptions, taken in isolation, may seem innocuous. The first says that 'bad products cannot drive out good', i.e. a high-quality product will hold onto some minimal market share no matter how many low-quality products it competes with. This assumption leads, by the end of Chapter 1, to the conclusion that the capabilities required to produce high-quality products will inevitably be 'scarce': the global market will be dominated by a small number of firms.

The key assumption driving Chapter 2 is that scarce capabilities tend to be clustered (in terms of geography). This assumption is familiar from the Geography and Trade literature – but here the agenda is different. By combining it with the key assumption of Chapter 1, we arrive at a theory of the currently popular 'product mix diagrams' that link a country's wealth to the mix of goods it produces and exports.

In Chapter 3 we introduce the last, and least controversial, of our key assumptions: you can't make something out of nothing. In other words, not all costs are labour costs. All manufactured exports require for their production some material inputs, whether in the form of raw material, components, or bought-in sub-assemblies. The central result of Chapter 3 is that this simple feature is enough to drive a wedge between the economics of 'productivity' and the economics of 'quality' . . . and in so doing, it makes clear why the new literature on Quality and Trade actually matters.

As the analysis of globalization continues through Chapters 4 and 5, we will be drawn into issues that require a deeper discussion of

insights into the role of quality and productivity heterogeneity. Finally, Grossman and Helpman's (1991) quality-ladder model provides a dynamic link between quality, trade, and growth.

'capabilities' than that set out in Chapter 1, and it is at this point that we ask: what are the basic determinants of firms' capabilities? How can these capabilities be developed? And how can they be transferred across firms and countries? And what do these answers imply about Industrial Development in a globalizing world?

1

Capabilities

1.1. THE WEALTH OF NATIONS

Ever since Adam Smith wrote the Wealth of Nations, one of the central questions of economics has been, why are some countries richer or poorer than others? Answers abound: in the 1960s, the standard response was that rich countries had more capital stock (i.e. 'machinery') than poor countries; and this larger capital stock had its origin in the savings made by earlier generations. In the 1990s, the standard response was that rich countries had a better set of legal and social institutions, which provided an environment within which businesses could thrive, and the roots of these institutions ran deep into a country's history. The popularity of different answers sometimes reflected the salience of recent experience: the 1990s focus on institutions grew out of the apparent failure of the former Soviet Union countries to respond to the overnight liberalization of (capital) markets introduced at the beginning of the decade. Some answers were better than others: the 'capital stock' story is not without merit, but if that was the whole story, the poverty of Sub-Saharan Africa could have been solved three times over by devoting half a century of aid money to the purchase of machines. One of the most poignant moments on British TV came in the middle of Peter Jay's series on 'The Road to Riches'; see Jay (2001). Walking through a Tanzanian cashew nut factory built with World Bank money, so that home-grown produce could be processed locally, he found himself alone, among the perfectly functioning machinery.

So what of all the explanations? Clearly, we're in complex terrain here. Many things matter, and their separate influences may be deeply intertwined. But there is one way forward that allows us to separate out two stages of the analysis in a useful way.

My point of departure lies in distinguishing between *proximate* and *ultimate* causes of differences in wealth. The proximate cause lies, for the most part,[1] in the capabilities of firms. The ultimate causes, whether they be human capital, institutions, or otherwise, lead to economic growth through one central channel: by raising the volume and quality of output produced by the country's firms from the inputs available to them. This is almost a truism, since all that's involved in this claim is a restatement of the old adage: productivity determines GDP per capita. So let's start there . . .

1.2. THE WIDGET MAKERS

Imagine that the world consists of a bunch of different countries, in each of which people spend some of their time making widgets. Everyone in the world loves widgets; it's the only thing they spend money on. Every country has its own colour, blue or green, and its citizens can make only that colour. Half of all the widgets made in the world are blue, and half are green.

But when it comes to 'consuming' widgets, everyone likes to have an even mix of colours. They'll swap a blue for a green, or vice versa, on a one-for-one basis, to get an even mix. But they don't mind all that much, and if they're asked to swap at a less favourable rate, they will say no.

The outcome is that widgets get swapped across country boundaries, until everyone has the mix they want. This constitutes 'trade'. Now for 'productivity': people in some countries are quicker or more industrious than others, and they produce more widgets in a year: their 'productivity' is higher. So is their wealth. The number of widgets they end up with after doing all their swaps is the same as they produced. For individuals, and for countries, productivity determines wealth.

Of course you could say I'm only talking about proximate causes. Why Mr Smith, or Lithuania, has a higher or lower level of productivity goes back to Mr Smith's difficult childhood, or Lithuania's cultural heritage. Yes, it does; and we'll talk about these deeper questions

---

[1] The only major qualifications are (i) that this statement takes as given each country's endowment of human capital and natural resources, and (ii) that the size and productivity of the non-market (public) sector of the economy also affects outcomes.

underlying productivity and quality in Chapters 4 and 5. But for now, productivity determines GDP/capita: we're talking 'only' about the proximate causes of wealth. The reason this is worth focussing on, is that whatever are the deep and 'true' causes of wealth differences, they can only affect wealth insofar as they affect productivity. Productivity is the channel through which these things affect wealth.

So what's missing in the world of widgets? A lot, obviously. But the bits I want to focus on are quite simple and straightforward: I want to expand the set of goods from the simple widgets to all kinds of goods. And I want to show that the features of goods that will matter to my present story are simple in the extreme. By the end of this chapter, we'll have arrived at a restatement of the link from productivity to wealth, within the richer framework of 'capabilities'. With that aim in mind, let's start with a firm that makes some superior class of widget …

1.3. THE FIRM

In a market economy, a firm's viability depends on its earning a flow of profit that is at least as valuable as the costs it has incurred in establishing its business. Those costs are of many kinds: building a factory, inventing or developing a product, even building up a brand image. All that is in the past; we take a snapshot of the firm as a functioning entity, competing in the marketplace with its very superior widgets. What determines the flow of profit it can generate? Only two things can matter, once we've reduced things to this simple scenario: one is the number of labour hours it takes to make a widget; we'll assume, realistically, that that's a constant, independently of the number of units produced: call it c. Then, if w denotes the hourly wage rate, the production cost of a widget is wc. It is useful to take the number of widgets produced per hour, which is $1/c$, as our measure of the firm's productivity level.

How much can you sell a very superior widget for? The higher the price you quote, the fewer you sell. Raising the quality of the widget means that at any given price, you'll sell more units. By the same token, for any sales volume you're aiming at, you can support a higher price. Quality, in other words, is a 'demand shifter'. Using the same language, productivity is a 'cost shifter'.

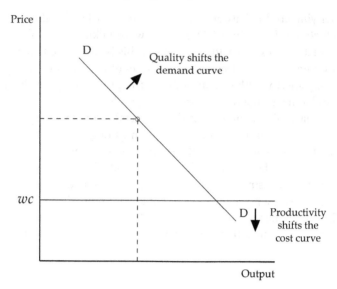

Fig. 1.1. Demand Shifters and Cost Shifters

It sounds simple, but it's a powerful formalism. It immediately throws a very broad meaning onto the word 'quality'. In all that follows, 'quality' refers to anything that shifts the demand schedule outwards: technical characteristics, after sales service, brand image, and so on ... as we'll see in Box 1.2 below.

The great advantage of wrapping up these disparate elements of product quality into a 'demand shifter', is that (a) for many purposes, they all have the same effect, and lumping them together is harmless; and (b) we now get a simple statement: no matter how complex a market we insert this firm into, the only things that can affect its profit flow, and so the viability of this business, are the two parameters representing the cost shifter and the demand shifter. We'll refer to the cost shifter as productivity, and we'll represent it by $1/c$. (Sometimes we'll use the label c, rather than $1/c$, in the interests of keeping the notation simple.) The demand shifter will be referred to as 'quality', and we'll label it as u.

It's this pair of numbers that we'll refer to as the firm's 'capability' in the market for widgets. More generally, we'll refer to the firm's capability by asking what values u and c take in each of the markets in which it operates, or might operate. (This richer description in terms of a *set* of (u, c) values is explored in the next chapter.) We'll think of these markets as being narrowly defined ('widgets' rather than 'engineering components') so that the u and c can be thought of as referring to a specific product (or product line). But that's all that's to it for the moment.

When I use the word 'capability' in this way, I am using shorthand for what I might more properly refer to as the firm's 'revealed capability', i.e. the observable outcome of the firm's underlying capability. In the Managment literature, the term capability is used to refer to these deeper attributes of the firm, which are (often) not directly observable or measurable (Box 1.1).

Of course, it's tempting to ask at once about these deeper attributes: where do the u and c come from? We will reach this level of discussion in Chapter 4, but we begin in this chapter with the idea that it's the firm's past efforts and investments that have left it with its current values of u and c...and we ask, given some set of firms in today's market, with their various levels of u and c, how will competition between them pan out?

Box 1.1. The Roots of Capabilities

The term 'capability' is used in the main text as shorthand for what might better be called 'revealed capability', i.e. the performance-relevant outcome of the firm's underlying capabilities. This begs the question: what is the nature of these underlying 'capabilities'?

The primary point to be made here is that the 'interesting' elements of this underlying capability are those elements that can't be bought 'off the shelf', i.e. those to which all firms have free access on the market. This idea lies at the core of the 'Resource Based Theory of the Firm' literature, which traces its roots to Penrose (1959), via Rumelt (1984), Wernerfelt (1984) and Lockett, Thompson, and Morgenstern (2009).

More recently, the literature of 'organizational capital' has attempted to unearth the factors that lead one firm to achieve higher levels of productivity and quality than its rivals. (For a review, see Gibbons and Henderson (2011).)

These are difficult questions. One of the central problems in addressing the issues involved, is that differences in the performance (profitability) of firms will usually be driven both by factors internal to the firm (our focus of interest here), and by external factors, i.e. the different market environment in which different firms operate. Unravelling these two kinds of influence is notoriously difficult. To address this issue, some researchers have focussed on groups of closely comparable firms, between which differences in the external environment are both small, and identifiable (so that they can be controlled for in an econometric study). Thus, interest has focussed on such groups as restaurants belonging to the same chain (Gibbons and Henderson (2011)), or the set of all ready-mix concrete plants in a city (Hortaçsu and Syverson (2007), Syverson (2008)).

Box 1.1. **(continued)**

The latter setting is of particular interest here, as it illustrates one influence that can be central to performance differences. Ready-mix concrete plants supply concrete, shipped in trucks, to construction sites in a local area (usually a city). The concrete, once prepared, must be delivered quickly. The main attribute that distinguishes high-performing from low-performing depots is the effectiveness with which they manage the complex and demanding set of decisions about scheduling deliveries. As Syverson (2008) remarks: 'Ready-mix concrete producers are not just manufacturers, they are logisticians: they deliver, typically on short notice, a perishable product to time-sensitive buyers in multiple locations.' This is the task of a team comprising a handful of individuals, and the skill of one individual (team leader) is a crucial determinant of performance. So, in this instance, the capability of the 'firm' rests to a high degree on the skills of a single individual.

Moving one step up in terms of organizational complexity, we have the law firms studied by Garicano and Hubbard (2005, 2007, 2009). Here, lawyers of differing levels of ability are sorted into different roles, and a firm's capability rests on the 'architecture' of its organization.

It is the extension and elaboration of such ideas, in more complex settings, that underlies the recent literature on 'Organizational Capital' (Prescott and Visscher (1980), Atkeson and Kehoe (2005)).

This literature identifies one key source of a firm's value in the organizational structure of the firm, as opposed to its proprietary knowledge, or its market position. (In other words, with the assembling of a team of people who work effectively together, within some framework of rules, routines and tacit understandings that have been put in place or have evolved over time.) To see what this implies, consider, for example, the Aquafresh company in Ghana (Sutton and Kpenty (2012)). This company began life in the clothing and textiles sector, but when this sector came under intense competition from Chinese imports, the firm reinvented itself as a maker of soft drinks. Its expertise in clothing and textiles was secondary to the fact that it was a well-functioning midsize firm, that could reorient itself in the product market as market circumstances changed.

A more general perspective on this issue emerges from the work of Peter Schott, Andrew Bernard, Steven Redding, and Bradford Jensen, who have studied the way in which US industries adapt to competition from low-wage countries. Key to their results is that a primary survival mechanism lies in switching the balance of a firm's activities towards new product lines. See Bernard, Jensen, and Schott (2006), Bernard, Redding, and Schott (2010, 2011).

1.4. COMPETING IN CAPABILITIES

Suppose we have a number of competing firms, each characterized by its levels of c and u. When competition occurs between these differently placed firms, what happens?

Some will be 'active': they will produce some level of output, and have a price that exceeds their level of unit cost (and so have positive profit margins). The remaining firms will be 'inactive' in the sense that they will be unable to sell any quantity of output at a price sufficient to cover their unit costs of production. How does this happen? Consumers will buy a product only if it offers a price – quality combination that is as good as that offered by rival firms. So there will be some threshold in terms of the price – quality combination that firms must reach in order to survive. If a firm's quality is low, or its productivity is poor, then, even if it cuts its price to the level of its unit cost, pushing its profit margin to zero, it may still offer an unacceptable price – quality combination. Such a firm will remain inactive.

So we are left with the outcome where some sets of firms will be active, and their prices will vary with their respective quality levels, while their profit margins will vary both with their quality levels and their productivity (and so cost) levels.

How good a 'capability level' does a firm need in order to be active? Given the equilibrium prices ground out by competition between the active firms, there will be a curve in the space of quality, u, and productivity, $1/c$, above which a potential entrant to the market needs to be. An illustration of this threshold level is shown in Figure 1.2.

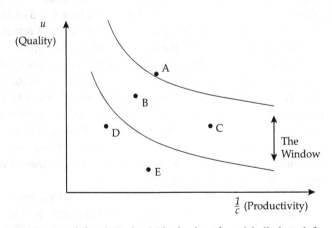

Fig. 1.2. The Capability 'Window'. The leading firm, labelled A, defines the top of the window. Its active rivals are B and C, while firms D and E are inactive. The process of competition between A, B and C determines equilibrium prices, and so fixes the bottom of the window, i.e. a curve in $(u, 1/c)$ space below which a firm will sell zero at equilibrium ('be inactive').

All active firms have a capability level that lies between the highest level in the market and threshold level needed for entry. I will refer to the band lying between these two curves as the 'window': to be an active firm, you need to get your capability level into this window. (Figure 1.2.)

1.5. THE FIRST KEY ASSUMPTION: BAD PRODUCTS CANNOT DRIVE OUT GOOD

Consider an industry comprising a number of firms, indexed by i, where c_i and u_i denote, respectively, the productivity and quality parameters of firm i. We describe the demand side of the market as follows: all consumers have the same utility function, of the form

$$U = (ux)^\delta z^{1-\delta} \tag{1.1}$$

Here, z denotes the individual's consumption of some 'outside good'; we focus on the good quantity purchased in our market of interest; here, the quantity purchased is x and the quality offered by the firm supplying the good is u. It follows from the form of the Cobb–Douglas utility function that consumers spend a fixed fraction $1 - \delta$ of their income on the outside good, independently of prices and qualities, and so the remaining fraction in the market is what concerns us here. It is convenient to denote total consumer expenditure in this market by a constant, S. The second feature of this utility function is that the consumer will choose the product, or one of the several products, that offer the best quality – price ratio.[2] It follows that, at equilibrium, all firms that are active, in the sense of having strictly positive sales revenue, must have the same, i.e. the equal-highest, quality – price ratio. This demand system also has a second, less obvious feature that will play a crucial role in all that follows.

The easiest way to introduce this feature is to consider a setting in which all the firms have the same productivity parameter, and so the same unit cost of production. Quality levels, however, are different, in that one firm has a 'higher' quality u while all the other firms

---

[2] To see this, note that spending S on firm i's product yields S/p_i units of quality u_i and so the bracketed term in (1.1) equals Su_i/p_i.

have a 'lower' quality $v < u$. Now imagine some form of competition between the firms. (We will be looking at Cournot competition, but for the moment any other form, such as Bertrand competition, for example, will do. The feature we're about to encounter is a feature of the demand system per se, and does not reflect the use of any particular form of competition between the firms.) The one thing we can say, for any form of competition in which firms are standard 'profit-maximizers', is that firms will not price below their unit cost of production, and so earn negative profits (as they will always have an available action that leaves them with zero output and zero profit). This in turn means that the 'worst' scenario that can be faced by the 'higher' quality producer is that all its 'lower' quality rivals sell at a price that exactly coincides with the level of unit costs (unit marginal cost), which is, as we assumed, the same for all firms. But this in turn means that our 'higher quality' firm will always enjoy a price strictly greater than this common level of marginal cost, and correspondingly (positive) levels of output, sales revenue, and market share (defined as its sales revenue divided by total industry sales revenue, which in this setting equals S, as we noted earlier).

Now let's step back from the 'worst case scenario', and ask, how could such a scenario be reached? One story of interest here is one in which the number of 'lower quality' rivals increases over time; and as they enter the market in greater numbers, competition between them forces their common price down to the level of their common marginal cost. This process of entry may damage the profits, and reduce the market share, of the 'higher quality' firm – but as our discussion of 'worst case scenario' shows, it cannot drive that firm's market share to zero. There is a minimal market share that the 'higher quality' firm must retain, no matter how many 'lower quality' rivals it faces.

In other words, a 'higher quality' producer cannot be squeezed out of the market by 'lower quality' rivals, no matter how many such rivals appear. Now this may seem obvious – and indeed it is so plausible and natural an account of how things work in practice that this whole discussion may seem belaboured. But viewed against the context of the modern literature, this point really is of central importance. To see why, suppose we started instead with the standard 'constant elasticity of substitution' (CES) utility function. Whether we use it in its original form, as introduced by Dixit and Stiglitz and adapted to the International Trade literature by Krugman, or its extended various forms; it carries the central property that *all* firms' market shares will be eroded to zero as the number of rival firms increases indefinitely.[3]

Now the property that good products cannot be squeezed out by bad is not special to the utility function (1.1) above. Rather, it is a general feature of the wide class of models that provide a basis for the modern theory of market structure (Sutton (2007a)). It is essential to any account of why many industries around the world remain dominated by a small number of firms, despite the huge size of the global market – as we will see below. It is also an extremely plausible, indeed compelling, property of actual markets. But on a purely theoretical level, it is a substantial assumption.

The central theme of this chapter lies in exploring the consequences of this assumption that 'bad products cannot drive out good' ... and the central result of the chapter is that this leads to the first of our key implications: some capabilities will always, necessarily, be 'scarce'.

It is time to move on. Having put in place the demand system defined by (1.1), we need to complete our description of the model by specifying the form of competition. Here, I'll use the most conventional form, namely Cournot competition (i.e. a Nash equilibrium in quantities).[4] Each firm sets a quantity of output. The quantity may be zero, in which case we say the firm is 'inactive'. All active firms have prices proportional to their qualities, i.e. p_i/u_i is the same for all active firms. We use the label λ to denote this common value of p_i/u_i. Given the quantities set by the firms, the value of λ is set to equate supply and demand in the market – and it is this that fixes the level of prices in the market. Given this mechanism to fix prices, each firm takes rivals' quantities as given, and chooses its own quantity to maximize profit. (In other words, this is the standard story we tell about how a Cournot equilibrium works, except for the complication that firms differ in the quality of their products.)

So what happens?

---

[3] This model dominated the International Trade literature throughout the 1980s and 1990s. The central feature of Sutton (2007b) is that it departs from this framework.

[4] Combining (1.1) with Cournot Competition define the 'Cournot Model with Quality' introduced by Sutton (1991), on which all the analysis that follows is based.

Box 1.2. Demand Shifters

In 'short-run' analysis (Sections 1.2 to 1.4), we take as given the capabilities of the firm, as represented by its demand and cost shifter for each narrowly defined market (in which it may or may not operate). In 'long run' analysis (Section 1.9), we look at the investments the firm makes in moving its demand and cost shifters.

So long as we are confining attention to the short run then, the demand and cost shifters of all firms active in the market suffice in themselves to fully determine the flow of profit accruing to each firm. This offers a powerful general framework – since all we now need to know is the $(u, 1/c)$ pairs. On the other hand, it hides a multitude: for we have deliberately defined the cost and demand shifters in such a general way that their values may reflect a very wide range of influences.

While the cost shifter is relatively easy to conceptualize, the demand shifter is more complex. It is often convenient to refer to the demand shift variable u as 'quality', but this is just shorthand for perceived quality, i.e. consumers' willingness-to-pay. Thus it includes not just 'quality' in the usual narrow sense (a feature of the product's physical characteristics), but also a range of characteristics that include, for example:

- brand advertising: for example, a major Indian tractor manufacturer is currently working to establish its tractors in the US market. Success will hinge just as much on customer perceptions, as on technical performance.

- services: for a machine tool maker, the network of service engineers available to repair the machines may be of similar importance to buyers as the machine's engineering characteristics.

- logistics: for a maker of clothing in the Far East selling to a UK department store, the ability to alter designs and deliver consignments at very short notice is just as important as the physical characteristics of the garment itself.

1.6. THE WINDOW

To see what happens, we begin by calculating the equilibrium level of output, price, and profit of some particular firm, labelled firm i. Let the unit wage level[5] faced by firm i be denoted w_i, and the number

---

[5] If all firms operate in the same (competitive) labour market, then w_i will be the same for all, and we may drop the subscript i. However, we will be interested, in later chapters, in markets in which the competing firms operate in different countries, with different wage rates.

of units of labour (the only variable input) per unit of output be c_i, so that marginal cost is $w_i c_i$ and firm i's profit[6] at output level x_i is

$$\Pi_i = p_i x_i - w_i c_i x_i$$

Now since

$$p_j = \lambda u_j \text{ for all firms}, j = 1 \text{ to } n, \qquad (1.2)$$

and since the value of output in the market, $\sum p_j x_j$, equals consumer expenditure in the market S, it follows that, using (1.2),

$$\sum p_j x_j = \lambda \sum u_j x_j = S$$

or

$$\lambda = \frac{S}{\sum u_j x_j}$$

whence

$$p_i = \lambda u_i = \frac{u_i S}{\sum u_j x_j} \qquad (1.3)$$

and so firm i's profit can be written as a function of its output x_i.

Firm i sets x_i to maximize

$$\Pi_i = p_i x_i - w_i c_i x_i$$
$$= (u_i S / \sum u_j x_j - w_i c_i) x_i$$

taking $x_1, \ldots, x_{i-1}, x_{i+1}, \ldots, x_n$ as given.

A routine calculation, which is set out in Appendix 1.1, yields the Nash equilibrium solution for the firms' outputs and prices, given their capabilities. It is convenient to adopt the shorthand notation k_j to represent the ('effective cost') indicator, $w_j c_j / u_j$, and to express the solution in terms of quality-adjusted prices and outputs as follows: for any firm i with positive output at equilibrium (an 'active firm'):

$$\frac{p_i}{u_i} = \frac{1}{n-1} \sum_{\substack{j \text{ st } x_j > 0}} k_j \qquad (1.4)$$

and its (quality-adjusted) output is

---

[6] All fixed costs incurred in entering the market are sunk, and do not enter Π_i.

$$u_i x_i = S \frac{n-1}{\displaystyle\sum_{j \, st \, x_j > 0} k_j} \left[1 - (n-1) \frac{k_i}{\displaystyle\sum_{j \, st \, x_j > 0} k_j} \right] \qquad (1.5)$$

so long as the term in [·] is non-negative, and zero otherwise. In the former case, firm i's equilibrium profit equals

$$\Pi_i = S\pi_i = \left[1 - (n-1) \frac{k_i}{\displaystyle\sum_{j \, st \, x_j > 0} k_j} \right]^2 S \qquad (1.6)$$

and n denotes the number of firms that are active at equilibrium, and where we have introduced the notation π_i to represent firm i's profit in a market of size $S = 1$.

The boxed output and profit equations (1.5) and (1.6) are of central and continuing importance in all that follows; indeed, the central analytical results of later chapters will require little more than the repeated use, in new contexts, of the output equation (1.5).

The shape of the profit function (1.6) is illustrated in Figure 1.3.

Consider first the case where firm i's effective cost level k_i is equal to the mean level for all firms $\sum k_j/n$. Inserting this into the profit formula (1.6) yields $\Pi_i = S/n^2$. This is shown as point A in Figure 1.3.

As firm i's effective cost level falls indefinitely, its profit rises asymptotically to S as its market share approaches unity. (Point B in Figure 1.3.)

The key feature is shown as point C in the figure: as k_i rises to a critical level, Π_i falls to zero. This is the 'lower threshold' mentioned in the preceding section. We can calculate the value of k_i to which this corresponds by simple inspection of the profit formula (1.6) (or the output formula (1.5)). The term in the bracket [·] falls to zero when

$$(n-1)k_i = \sum k_j = k_i + \sum_{j \neq i} k_j$$

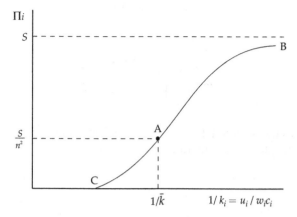

Fig. 1.3. Equilibrium profit Π_i as a function of $1/k_i$. The parameter $k_i = w_i c_i / u_i$ represents firm i's effective cost level. The diagram is drawn in terms of $1/k_i$ so that a rightward movement corresponds to a rise in quality u_i, or a rise in productivity, $1/c_i$.

or when

$$(n-2)k_i = \sum_{j \neq i} k_j \tag{1.7}$$

where the sums are taken over j such that $x_j > 0$. We can interpret this more easily by noting that the $n - 1$ (active) rival firms have a mean value of effective cost k_j equal to

$$\left(\sum_{j \neq i} k_j \right) / (n-1).$$

Writing this mean value of rivals' effective costs as $\bar{k}$, (1.7) can be written as

$$k_i = \frac{n-1}{n-2}\bar{k} \tag{1.7'}$$

or

$$\frac{1}{k_i} = \frac{n-2}{n-1}\frac{1}{\bar{k}} \tag{1.7''}$$

which says that i's effective cost k_i can lie above $\bar{k}$ by at most this ratio $\frac{n-1}{n-2}$ (>1). This constitutes the first of two key propositions:

Proposition 1 (The Short Run Proposition)

For any set of n firms with effective cost levels k_j, there is a threshold level of effective cost above which a firm cannot achieve positive sales revenue at equilibrium.

1.7. THE VIABILITY CONDITION EXPLORED

In view of the central role played by the viability condition (1.7) in later chapters, it is worth pausing at this point to examine the condition more closely. In writing down (1.7), we began by looking at a context in which there were n firms, all of which had strictly positive output at equilibrium, and we focussed on one of these firms, labelled firm i, and asked: at what threshold value of k_i would x_i fall to zero? This threshold value is defined by the equality (1.7).

An alternative way of representing the threshold for viability is to imagine a potential entrant to the market. Denote by n_0 the number of incumbent firms, all with strictly positive output levels, and label the potential entrant as firm $n_0 + 1$. The threshold level of k_{n_0+1} below which this potential entrant can achieve positive sales revenue is given by equation (1.7): note that we can identify firm i in (1.7) as our potential entrant, remembering that the sum on the r.h.s. is taken over firm i's rivals, which in this context are the n_0 incumbent firms, while the total number of firms has become $n_0 + 1$. Hence, the viability threshold for our potential entrant is

$$k_{n_0+1} = \frac{1}{n_0 - 1} \sum_{j=1}^{n_0} k_j \qquad (1.8)$$

This form of the viability condition for a potential entrant will be used in later chapters.

The preceding discussion may raise the following question: when we write down the viability condition, which firms are to be included in the summation? We have chosen to define the condition (1.7) by reference to the sum over firms whose output is *strictly* positive. It is obvious that the capability values of these firms affect the threshold. It is also obvious that the presence of firms whose capability values lie *strictly* above the threshold defined by (1.7) cannot affect the value of the threshold itself; these firms produce zero output, and have no effect on equilibrium prices. But what about firms that are exactly on the margin of viability, in the sense that their capability coincides exactly with the threshold value defined by (1.7)? It seems obvious, intuitively, that since their equilibrium value of output is zero, they cannot affect the value of the threshold. A simple calculation, set out in Appendix 1.3, shows that this is indeed the case.

This observation justifies our use of the strict inequality $x_j > 0$ in defining the number of firms to be counted in the formula for the viability threshold. It also shows that including firms that are exactly on the margin of viability is harmless: we obtain the same answer whether these firms are included in the summation or not.

1.8. THE OUTPUT EQUATION REVISITED

Now that we have explored the viability condition, it is helpful to digress briefly in order to point out some properties of the key output equation (1.5), on which much of our later analysis will rest.

We summarize the relevant properties in Lemma 1 below, the proof of which is given in Appendix 1.2. The key point to note about these results is that they refer to the way in which a firm's effective cost level $k_j = w_j c_j / u_j$ affects its equilibrium output *over a particular domain*. This domain is defined by the viability condition. Specifically, we are concerned here with a firm whose effective cost level lies between the (high) threshold level it must go below in order to attain viability, and the average effective cost level of the incumbent firms in the market. (This will be of interest in the next chapter, where we will be looking at a 'low quality' firm attempting to enter the market.)

Now what Lemma 1 says is that, over this domain, a reduction in a firm's effective cost level raises its equilibrium output (properties 1 and 2), while – less obviously[7] – a rise in quality that is fully offset by a proportional increase in (wage) costs will lead to a fall in output.

It will be useful, for further reference, to note some properties of the function.

---

[7] The proportionate changes in quality and the wage rate leave the effective cost level unchanged. From equation (1.5), this leaves profit unchanged, as π_i depends on w_i and u_i only via their ratio, $k_i = w_i c_i / u_i$. But inspection of the output equation (1.5) shows that the quality-adjusted output level $u_i x_i$ is a function of k_i – but x_i is *not* invariant to changes in u_i and w_i that leaves k_i fixed.

Lemma 1 *On the domain where the inequality*

$$\frac{w_i c_i}{u_i} < \frac{1}{n-1} \sum_j \frac{w_j c_j}{u_j} = \frac{n}{n-1} \left(\overline{\frac{w_j c_j}{u_j}} \right)$$

holds, so that $x_i > 0$:

1. $\dfrac{\partial x_i}{\partial w_i} < 0.$

2. $\dfrac{\partial x_i}{\partial u_i} > 0.$

3. *A rise in u_i and w_i that leaves u_i/w_i unchanged implies a fall in x_i.*

These results follow immediately from the form of the output function. (The proofs are given in Appendix 1.2.)

So why is the domain restriction needed? Why are the rather obvious-looking properties 1 and 2 not valid everywhere? To see the intuition behind this, think of a new entrant to the market, whose quality rises over time (so that its effective cost level falls). Now initially, this will indeed lead to a rise in its equilibrium output level. But what will happen as its quality level rises far above that of any rival firm? Its rivals become less and less effective competitors; the ratio of their prices to that of the now high-quality entrant falls to zero. As this happens, the high-quality firm's position will become close to that of a monopolist; and in the present model, the monopoly solution involves setting an arbitrarily high price and an arbitrarily low output level. This suggests the intuition that underlies the domain restriction in Lemma 1: It is *not* the case, in general, that rising capability implies higher output. But over the domain defined in Lemma 1, which is the relevant domain to consider in analysing a low-quality/high-cost entrant that is engaged in 'catching up' on its rivals, it is indeed the case that rising capability implies rising output. This result will play an important role in Chapter 2.

1.9. THE LONG RUN

Up to this point, we have taken each firm's capability to be fixed, i.e. determined by investments or efforts undertaken by the firm in the past. The second of the two basic propositions relates to the 'long run'. It addresses the question: suppose firms were in a position to invest in improving their capabilities. Then, foreseeing the competitive environment we have just described, how many firms would invest in capability building, and to what level?

The 'long run' question is central in what follows, and it raises a number of complex issues. In order to set the scene, however, it is useful to begin with a rather abstract discussion, which sets aside all the details of the capability building process that will occupy us in the next section. With that in mind, suppose that the firm has access to some 'R&D' process that will allow it to improve the quality u_i of its product, or to raise its productivity $1/c_i$, for some fixed financial outlay. A higher level of u, or a lower level of c, just requires a correspondingly higher fixed outlay on 'R&D activity'.

It's worth noting what we are *not* dealing with here. Suppose a seller of the felt-tip pen with which I'm writing this paragraph decided to double the amount of ink in each pen. This is a quality increase, and will shift the demand curve outwards, as I discover these pens now last longer. But the firm needs to incur double the old level of cost on the ink, and so the firm's marginal cost schedule rises too: this type of quality change does *not* fall within the scope of the result I'm about to describe. But suppose my pen-maker employed a design house to advise him, and they suggested a redesign of the tip that stopped me ending each writing session with inky fingers: there is no change in the unit cost of production, a one-off payment to the design house, and all pens are better ... in this instance, the rise in capability involves a rise in *fixed* (and sunk) outlays.[8]

Now within this latter setting, a fundamental result holds; and the practical importance of this result derives in part from the fact that we have said nothing about *how* the rise in capability can be brought about. All that matters is that it involves a fixed (and sunk) cost, i.e. one that has nothing to do with the firm's current size (or level of output). Rather, it represents something like the development of a new product design, or the discovery of a new and better arrangement of

[8] But of course things are never this simple in practice: every design change carries *some* implications for unit costs, and it may involve either a rise or a fall. So it's worth noting that the simple case I'm describing here turns out to be of broad applicability. It will apply to cases where either (a) the fixed outlay leads to a fall in unit cost of production, with no change on the demand side; or (b) the fixed outlay leads to a rise in demand, with at most a *small* rise in unit costs (readers who are interested in pursuing what exactly 'small' means here may wish to refer to Sutton (1991), pp. 70–1 for the details).

the production process. Once learned, it can be implemented across any number of units of output that the firm produces. This is true of all the ways of 'raising capabilities' that we will explore in later chapters: the differences and details of how the change in capability is achieved, are immaterial, beyond the simple requirement that it involves only some 'one-off' expenditure of money and/or effort on the part of the firm to bring it about.[9]

Now think of a group of firms contemplating how much to spend on this kind of 'capability building' exercise. The right amount to spend will clearly depend on how much rival firms are spending. A certain number of firms will play the game, and invest in building capability. Others will hold back, and drop out. Our focus is on the number of capability-builders, who will constitute the 'active firms' of Figure 1.2.

The central result we develop below has a paradoxical flavour: the harder it is to build capability, the greater the number of firms in the market. Why?

The reason behind this result goes to the heart of the underlying economics. Suppose the cost outlay required to get from a lower-quality level v to a higher-quality level u is low. Then it might seem that more firms will be willing to pay the price and move up from v to u. But by the same token, it may then be worth moving not just to u, but to some higher quality (call it u^*). So there's a tension here: as it becomes cheaper to move up the quality spectrum, more firms would like to make any given move – but for the same reason, any single firm would want to move up higher (to u^*, or u^{**}, or u^{***}...), whatever the level chosen by its rivals. And it turns out that this second effect wins out. Instead of inducing more firms to move up a little, the access to cheaper ways of building capability has the effect of encouraging a *smaller* number of firms to stay in the game – but this smaller number of players will each spend *more*. Making capability-building cheaper means a *smaller* number of firms each spends *more* on their capability building efforts. That's the paradox.

The second thing that emerges in this setting follows immediately from the story we've just told. It relates to the question: suppose the size of the (global) market got bigger (as happened when India and China brought down the trade barriers that had largely isolated them from global markets during the 1960s, 1970s, and early 1980s)–what

---

[9] Of course, over time, there will in general be a series of such fixed outlays, bringing us to successively higher levels of capability – but on each occasion, the firm pays some fixed fee in terms of money and/or effort to bring about the current improvement.

happens? The intuition we've just seen provides the right clue. As the size of the market gets bigger, we might expect it to support more and more producers. But as the market gets bigger, the extra profit available to the firm with the best design, or the top-performance product, rises – and this induces all firms to invest more in capability building. So instead of an ever-rising number of players in an ever-growing global economy, we have instead a group of players – who in some industries can be few in number – each spending more and more on its capability-building efforts as the global market expands.

The effect of this is most dramatic in those industries where there is a narrowly defined market in which all consumers want the same thing. A good example is the market for wide-body commercial jet aircraft. Here, the buyers are airlines, and their aim is simple: how to achieve the lowest carrying cost per passenger-mile. Throughout the first decades of jet age, from the 1960s to the 1980s, the best way to achieve this was to expand aircraft size. And so the major players – Lockheed, McDonnell, Douglas, Boeing, and Airbus – were involved in a decades-long game that ended with the survival of only two global players: Boeing and Airbus (Sutton (1998), Chapter 15).

At the other end of the spectrum are two kinds of industry in which the 'window' can accommodate, even in the long run, a very large number of players. The first of these corresponds to the case where 'capability building' is expensive. But in what sense? Think of the sugar industry. There's a given, readily available, technology for turning sugar beet or sugar cane into granulated sugar. How could a sugar maker improve its capability? There are ways of organizing production that will save labour – but there's fairly limited scope for this. And you might come up with some technical innovation that squeezes a bit more sugar out of a beet, or cane. Again, the scope is limited. And what of the demand side? Sugar is a pure chemical (sucrose). The (white) sugar on your table is 99 per cent pure. Purifying it to be 99.9999 per cent sucrose might be an interesting task for industrial chemists, but consumers don't care. So you could spend a great deal of 'fixed outlays' here for a minimal shift in your cost or demand schedules. The result: the global sugar industry supports a huge number of refiners. No one refiner can steal much market from others by outspending them in 'capability building'.

There's another kind of industry that also permits a huge number of firms to co-exit in the window. In this instance, the key lies in the fact that the product offerings in any market differ from each other in two quite distinct ways. So far we've focussed on the fact that producers differ in 'quality' – and everyone likes better 'quality'. But what of other features, like the body styling of a car, or the lyrics of a song? Some buyers will prefer one firm's offering, while others prefer a rival's ... even though both are offered at the same price. This is called 'horizontal' differentiation, as opposed to the 'vertical' (quality-improving) differentiation we've been considering up to now, and it arises in its simplest form in the context of geographical location. Given that the evening newspaper sells for the same price in all stores, I'll patronize the one in my own neighbourhood, just as you'll patronize the one closer to you.[10]

Now the practical setting where this 'horizontal' differentiation becomes most important is well illustrated by the case of scientific instruments. Take, for instance, flow-meters. These instruments are used to measure the flow of liquids in industrial plants. Many types exist, based on different scientific principles (electromagnetic, ultrasonic, and so on). Different types lend themselves better to different applications. In general chemical plants, the electromagnetic and ultrasonic types are good substitutes. In the oil industry, the ultrasonic is preferred at any price (oil doesn't conduct electricity, so the electromagnetic type just doesn't work). In a market like this, there's room for a very large number of players in the window: no process of capability building by makers of electromagnetic flow-meters can ever drive ultrasonic specialists out of the oil industry segment. So the window can be wide, and can accommodate a multitude of firms, in industries of this kind.[11]

---

[10] The contrast with 'quality', also known as 'vertical' differentiation, is that if prices are equal, *all* consumers will choose the better of the two products: its quality is unambiguously 'higher' – as with, say, the operating speed of a computer: if two equal price machines differ in nothing except operating speed, no one picks the slow one.

[11] There is one more possibility that is worth noting, for the sake of completeness. In the model that follows, we will assume, to keep things simple, that all individuals have the same income. If we allow for a range of incomes across consumers, then the window of viable qualities widens, as there is more room for low-quality products sold to low-income consumers. At the extreme, if we allow the range of incomes to extend downwards to zero, it is possible to obtain an equilibrium market structure in which a small number of 'high capability' firms have an (arbitrarily) large combined market share, while a large number of (arbitrarily) small firms remain viable, albeit with a very small combined market share. (See, for example, Shaked and Sutton (1983).)

1.10. WHY (SOME) CAPABILITIES ARE (RELATIVELY) SCARCE

In what follows, we develop this result within the special setting of the Cournot model with quality.[12] The easiest way to proceed is by setting up a 3-stage game, as illustrated in Figure 1.4.

The third stage of this game is simply the Cournot model with quality that we've seen already. The quality and productivity level of the firm, which are determined by decisions made at earlier stages, will fix each firm's (gross) profit level, as given by our profit function (1.9), i.e.

$$\Pi_i = S\pi_i = \left[1 - (n-1)\frac{k_i}{\displaystyle\sum_{j \; st \; x_j > 0} k_j} \right]^2 \cdot S \qquad (1.9)$$

Now this function, as we've seen, is symmetric in u_i and $1/c_i$, so we'll lose nothing at this point by just setting the values of c_i and w_i equal to 1 for all firms, $k_i = w_i c_i / u_i$ becomes $1/u_i$. The profit function can now be written

$$\Pi_i = \left[1 - (n-1)\frac{1/u_i}{\displaystyle\sum_{j \; st \; x_j > 0} 1/u_j} \right]^2 \cdot S \qquad (1.10)$$

Now we introduce a function $F(u)$ to represent the fixed and sunk outlays that must be incurred by any firm to achieve quality level u.

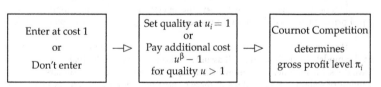

Fig. 1.4. The 3-stage game

---

[12] For a broad treatment, that allows for the presence of horizontal as well as vertical differentiation, see Sutton (1991), Chapter 3.

We'll take an iso-elastic function here, to keep things simple, setting

$$F(u) = u^\beta$$

so that

$$F(1) = 1$$

and

$$\frac{u}{F}\frac{dF}{du} = \beta$$

so that β represents the elasticity of F with respect to u (and $1/\beta$ is the elasticity of u with respect to F). A high value of β means that quality is relatively unresponsive to these cost outlays (which we may think of, for the moment, as R&D outlays – though we'll return to this point in Chapter 5, Box 5.1). A low value of β means that R&D spending is very effective in raising u – a relatively small outlay leads to a big rise in quality. (Figure 1.5.)

With this in hand, we can now come back to the structure of the 3-stage game of Figure 1.4.

Stage 1 is the entry stage, at which each of some ('large') number of potential entrants decides either to enter, and thereby incur a set-up cost of $F(1) = 1$, or not to enter. At stage 2, each firm decides whether

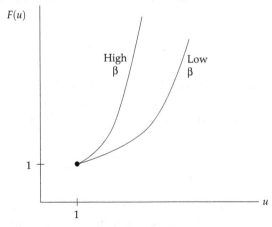

Fig. 1.5. The Fixed Cost Schedule $F(u) = u^\beta$ on $u \geq 1$.

to have a 'basic' quality of $u = 1$, or a higher quality $u > 1$. If it decides the latter, then it pays the incremental fee of $F(u) - F(1) = u^\beta - 1$.

We characterize equilibrium as a (subgame) perfect (pure strategy) Nash equilibrium of the 3-stage game. In other words, we proceed by backward induction, asking at stage 2 the question: Given the number n of firms that have entered at stage 1, what quality will they choose? We'll then go back to stage 1 and ask, given this relation between the number of entrants and the quality they will choose at stage 2, how many of the (large) number of potential entrants will enter?

We can characterize the equilibrium outcome by noting that it must satisfy two conditions. The first condition is that the level of quality u chosen by each firm at stage 2 must be optimal. This optimal configuration of the quality levels can take two forms. The first is one in which all firms set $u_i = 1$. Here, we require that the cost of raising u to any level $u > 1$ exceeds the gross profit gained by doing so. This gives us the (necessary) condition

$$\left.\frac{dF}{du_i}\right|_{u_j=1,\forall j} \geq \left.\frac{d\Pi_i}{du_i}\right|_{u_j=1,\forall j} \tag{1.11}$$

In what follows, we will distinguish two regimes, according as (1.11) is satisfied as a strict inequality ('regime I') or as an equality ('regime II'). We will show that the first regime corresponds to the case where market size S is small.

We begin with the second regime, where S is large. In this setting, we have an interior solution, where $u > 1$, and a necessary condition for equilibrium is that

$$\frac{dF}{du_i} = \frac{d\Pi_i}{du_i} \quad \text{for all } i \tag{1.12}$$

We seek a symmetric equilibrium, i.e. one in which all the u_j are equal at equilibrium. With this in mind, set $u_j = \bar{u}$ for all $j \neq i$, differentiate the profit function (1.10) with respect to u_i, and finally set $u_i = \bar{u}$ to obtain

$$\left.u_i\frac{d\Pi_i}{du_i}\right|_{u_i=\bar{u}} = 2\frac{(n-1)^2}{n^3}S \tag{1.13}$$

This is the first condition for equilibrium, in the regime where the (common) level of quality in the (symmetric) equilibrium of the stage 2 subgame exceeds unity.

We saw above that in the symmetric setting where all firms have the same quality $\bar{u}$, the value of $\Pi(\bar{u})$ is S/n^2, so that (1.13) implies

$$\frac{u_i}{\Pi_i}\frac{d\Pi_i}{du_i}\bigg|_{u_i=\bar{u}} = 2\frac{(n-1)^2}{n} \tag{1.14}$$

We now go back to stage 1, the entry stage. Here, it is convenient to begin by treating n as a continuous variable, so that the condition determining the equilibrium number n of entrants is the equality condition

$$\Pi(\bar{u}) = F(\bar{u}) \tag{1.15}$$

Combining (1.15) with equation (1.12) it follows that

$$\frac{u_i}{\Pi_i}\frac{d\Pi_i}{du_i}\bigg|_{u_i=\bar{u}} = \frac{u_i}{F}\frac{dF}{du_i}\bigg|_{u_i=\bar{u}} = \beta \tag{1.16}$$

so from (1.14) and (1.16) we have

$$\beta = 2\frac{(n-1)^2}{n}$$

or

$$n + \frac{1}{n} - 2 = \frac{\beta}{2} \tag{1.17}$$

Equation (1.17) is the key equilibrium describing market structure: it links the number of firms n that are active at equilibrium in this 'large market size' regime to the elasticity parameter β. We illustrate this in Figure 1.6.

So what we have established here is this: in a regime in which the firms choose a quality level strictly greater than 1, there will at equilibrium be a fixed number of entrants, independent of the size of the market: it is the absence of the market size parameter in Figure 1.6 which is the key point. The equilibrium number of firms depends on β alone, and not on S.

Before turning to the interpretation of this, we complete the analysis by pasting together the two possible regimes, and so describing the relation between market size and the equilibrium number of firms. (Figure 1.7.) In doing this, we'll replace the number of firms n with its reciprocal $1/n$, which is the conventional measure in the Industrial Organization literature. In the theoretical literature, the key summary measure of market structure is the share of industry sales accounted for by the largest firm, which is written as C_1 (the 'one-firm

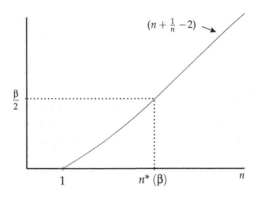

Fig. 1.6. The Equilibrium Number of Firms n^* as a Function of β.

concentration ratio'). In our present symmetric set-up, where all firms are of equal size at equilibrium, this is simply $1/n$.

Now for the market size vs market structure relationship. In Figure 1.7, we see that as market size S rises, the effect is to induce entry, as in the basic Cournot model. All firms set $u = 1$, and don't invest at stage 2. They each earn final stage profit S/n^2, and the number of entrants is fixed by the zero-profit condition, $S/n^2 = F(1) = 1$, whence $n = \sqrt{S}$. So as S rises, n rises, and $C_1 = 1/n$ falls. This is 'regime 1'.

The condition for being in regime 1 is that no firm wants to deviate by investing at stage 2 to achieve a quality level strictly greater than unity. This condition can be written as

$$\left.\frac{d\Pi_i}{du_i}\right|_{u_i=1} = \left.S\frac{d\pi_i}{du_i}\right|_{u_i=1} \leq \left.\frac{dF}{du_i}\right|_{u_i=1}$$

Using equation (1.13), this reduces to

$$u_i\frac{d\Pi_i}{du_i} = 2\frac{(n-1)^2}{n^3}S \leq \left.u_i\frac{dF}{du_i}\right|_{u_i=1} = \left.\beta u_i^\beta\right|_{u_i=1} = \beta$$

If we replace the inequality by an equality here, and insert the asymptotic value of n, which we labelled as $n^*(\beta)$ above, into the left-hand side expression, we obtain a critical value of S, which depends on β, at which we move from regime 1 to regime 2, as shown in Figure 1.7.

So what happens as S increases is that we reach a critical value of S, beyond which the effects of further increases in market size lead, not

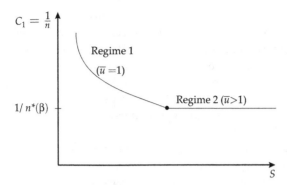

Fig. 1.7. Market Size and Concentration

to entry and falling concentration, but to an increasing escalation of expenditure on quality improvement. The bigger S, the higher is $\bar{u}$; but the number of firms remains unchanged.

So what of the dependence of n^*, and so $C_1 = 1/n^*$, on β? What we see from Figure 1.6 is that a fall in β leads to a fall in $n^*(\beta)$ and so to a rise in $C_1 = 1/n^*(\beta)$. This is the paradox: as it gets 'easier' to build quality, fewer firms do so. The resolution of the paradox lies in looking at it in a different way: a low value of β means that the quality improvement a firm gets for a given expenditure F is greater. Hence, the attractiveness to a deviant firm of outspending its rivals is greater. So escalation is more intense, and equilibrium spending is higher. It is an endogenous outcome of market forces that the industry becomes an increasingly expensive one to enter. In the language of our earlier discussion, a small number of firms build up capabilities that are relatively scarce.

This result constitutes the second of our two key propositions:

Proposition 2 (The Long Run Proposition)

Given any value of β, there is a corresponding lower bound to concentration, independently of the size of the market.

1.11. ROBUSTNESS

In the spirit of the present volume, the above discussion has been conducted in the special setting of the Cournot model. Its importance, however, lies in the fact that it illustrates a far more general result. All that is needed for this 'non-convergence' property to hold, is that our consumer utility (or demand) function conforms to the basis idea that 'bad qualities cannot drive out good'. Once this feature is present, we can extend and relax each of the special features of the example, and in particular the form of price competition, and the entry process. A full discussion of this is outside our scope, and the reader is referred to Sutton (1998) for the most general treatment (See also Symeonidis (2002)). There is, however, one point that is of fundamental interest in our present context: this relates to the way in which we can relax the form of the entry process.

Suppose, instead of our 3-stage game, we replace stages 1 and 2 with any finite sequence of stages; and then assign to each firm any stage at which it enters the game. As of that stage, the firm is free to enter, and make any investment it wishes. In other words, we can build in any 'historical' story we wish, giving any firm (or in the 'Trade' setting of later chapters, any country) an 'advantage' or 'disadvantage' of early or later entry into the (global) market, and the non-convergence result continues to hold. So this result captures something very robust and general about the outcome of a competitive market in which firms compete in qualities. More generally, while we have focussed on quality here, the argument relates more generally to capability: recall that, up to this point in our discussion, profit depends on quality u and productivity $1/c$ only via the ratio u/c, and so all that we have said about competition in quality carries over directly if we replace u with $1/c$, or with u/c. Competing in capabilities, in other words, involves a process in which, independently of the accidents of history, some capabilities will be 'scarce' – and it is this simple idea that will carry us forward to the next chapter, where we ask: where are these 'scarce' capabilities located, and why does it matter?

1.12. LOOKING AHEAD: A PREVIEW

With all this machinery in place, we can now sketch an informal outline of the way the globalization process will be represented in the chapters that follow.

If we flatten out the isoquants of Figure 1.2 by placing $\frac{u}{wc}$ on the vertical axis, and $1/wc$ on the horizontal axis, we obtain an alternative picture of the window, as shown in Figure 1.8, panel (i). In panel

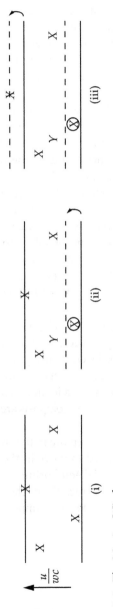

Fig. 1.8. The Moving Window

Notes: Panel (i) shows four viable producers, together with the u/wc 'window'. Panel (ii) shows the entry of a new firm Y into the global market, the consequent upward shift in the bottom of the window, and the exit of one of the original producers. Panel (iii) illustrates how changing incentives for long run investments move the top of the window upwards.

(ii) of the Figure, we illustrate the entry of a new producer from a country that has just opened up its borders to free trade. As it enters the window, two mechanisms come into play – and it is these mechanisms that drive the story in the chapters that follow.

First, the presence of the new firm makes price competition more intense, thus raising the threshold for viability (the bottom of the 'window') – and this may lead to the exit of some firms that were viable hitherto.

The second thing that will happen relates to firms' investments (in R&D or otherwise) that are aimed at improving their levels of quality (or productivity). As more firms enter the window, the market shares of all firms are reduced, and so the marginal returns to 'new' or 'incremental' investments in R&D aimed at raising their levels of quality (or productivity) will rise. Jumping ahead of the pack to obtain a large market share yields a greater incremental return. In the long run, as such investments are undertaken, the quality (or productivity) levels of some or all of the firms will rise – and so, in particular, the top level of $\frac{u}{wc}$ which serves to define the top of the window, will rise.[13] (The details of this argument, which brings us beyond the analysis of the present chapter, are discussed in Chapter 4.)

So the outcome of this 'globalization' process is a 'moving window' – as China's and India's producers enter the global market, they exert pressure on existing producers, leading to the exit of the least competitive, both in their home markets and in their export destinations. But they now find themselves in an increasingly competitive international environment, where the goalposts are constantly moving forwards ...

It is this story that we set out to explore in the chapters that follow – but before we can do so, we need to move in the next chapter from our present, single market, 'partial equilibrium' framework to a multimarket 'general equilibrium' setting. To set the ground for this, we conclude this chapter by looking at a very simple general equilibrium setting.

---

[13] Incidentally, these shifts will also, in general, lead to a further upward shift in the bottom of the window (not illustrated in Figure 1.8).

1.13. CAPABILITIES AND WEALTH

We end this chapter by looking at the relation between firms' capabilities and welfare. To do this, we need to extend the previous analysis by looking at equilibrium in the labour market, and so endogenizing the wage w, which we took as a given parameter faced by the firm in Section 1.2.

With this in mind, we consider a (single) country, in which there is a single industry of the kind modelled in Section 1.2, and a single wage rate w faced by all firms. We ignore the 'outside good', and let all individuals devote all their income to the purchase of this good. We extend the individual's utility function to incorporate labour supply, writing it as

$$U = ux - \frac{1}{2}l^2$$

This form has the property that the marginal utility of leisure, $\frac{dU}{dl}$, equals l – so the individual labour supply schedule will have the form of a ray through the origin, i.e. the volume of labour supplied will rise in direct proportion to the wage rate w, for any given level of prices and qualities.

The individual (or 'worker') supplies l units of labour at wage rate w, and spends income wl on x units of good of quality u sold at price p. The constrained maximization problem

$$\max_l U = ux - \frac{1}{2}l^2 \tag{1.18}$$

$$subject\ to\ px = wl$$

yields the solution

$$l = u \cdot \frac{w}{p} \tag{1.18a}$$

The consumer's budget constraint implies that the equilibrium level of consumption per capita is wl/p, and we will write this $\bar{x}$ (to distinguish it from the level of output per firm, which we continue to write as x). Substituting $\bar{x} = wl/p$ and $l = uw/p$ into (1.18) yields

$$U = \frac{1}{2}\left(u\frac{w}{p}\right)^2 \tag{1.19}$$

We now turn to the analysis of the firms. In this section, we focus on a symmetric set-up in which n firms offer the same quality u. Profits are distributed to a separate set of individuals ('non-workers'), who have the same utility function (1.18) but with l constrained to zero, i.e. $U = ux$. These firms face a market demand schedule of the form $p \sum_i x_i = S$, where S is total expenditure, as before.

In the present, symmetric, setting, the output per firm given by equation (1.5) reduces to (recall marginal cost in our present setting is wc):

$$x = \frac{n-1}{n^2} \frac{S}{wc} \qquad (1.20)$$

and equilibrium price is (from equation (1.4))

$$p = \frac{n}{n-1} cw \qquad (1.21)$$

Using (1.21) to substitute for w/p in (1.19) yields

$$U = \frac{1}{2} \left(\frac{n-1}{n} \right)^2 \left(\frac{u}{c} \right)^2$$

which gives the link between capability u/c and the individual worker's utility, which we will take as our welfare indicator.

What is the level of the real wage in this economy? We can define the real wage as the number of units of quality-adjusted output that can be exchanged for one unit of labour input. This is given by

$$\frac{w}{p/u}$$

From equation (1.21) we have

$$\frac{w}{p/u} = \frac{n-1}{n} \cdot \frac{u}{c}$$

This links capability u/c to the real wage.[14]

It remains to calculate the level of activity in the economy, which we measure as the total labour input at equilibrium. Denoting the

---

[14] The factor $(n-1)/n$ reflects the level of the price–cost margin, which is linked to the equilibrium return to past investment in capability building, as we saw in Section 1.9.

total number of workers by N, and using (1.18a), total labour supply equals

$$L^S = Nl^S = N \cdot u\frac{w}{p} \qquad (1.22)$$

which on substituting for w/p from (1.21) yields

$$L^S = N\frac{n-1}{n}\frac{u}{c} \qquad (1.23)$$

while labour demand is given by

$$L^D = ncx \qquad (1.24)$$

(remembering that x is per-firm output and one unit of output requires c units of labour output). Equating $L^S = L^D$ we find the value of per-firm output in terms of the primitives of the model,

$$x = N\frac{n-1}{n^2}\left(\frac{u}{c}\right)\frac{1}{c}$$

and equating this to the per-firm output equation (1.20) we obtain

$$\frac{1}{w}\cdot\frac{S}{N} = \frac{u}{c} \qquad (1.25)$$

We can interpret the l.h.s. expression as gross national expenditure per capita, expressed in wage units (i.e. using the wage rate as our numeraire).

What the equation tells us is that as capability $\frac{u}{c}$ rises, the real wage rises and, given our upward sloping labour supply function, the level of employment (and so output) expands, and so real GDP per capita rises.

Incidentally, equation (1.25) can be derived more directly: readers who are interested will find details in Appendix 1.4.

1.14. SUMMING UP

We began this chapter by introducing a model in which bad products cannot drive out good. This led us to the notion of a 'window' of capability within which a firm must lie in order to be viable. Competition to establish oneself in this window implies a shakeout of firms: in a long run equilibrium, some kinds of market will be dominated by a small number of firms. In other words, some capabilities will necessarily be relatively scarce, and so valuable. Finally, capabilities determine wealth – and in the next chapter, we extend this notion to a multi-country setting, in which the capabilities of a country's firms form the proximate determinant of its GDP per capita.

2

Wealth

2.1. THE SECOND KEY ASSUMPTION: CLUSTERING[1]

It has long been noted that as a country develops, its mix of activities, and the goods that it produces and exports, changes over time. The best way to see this process is by looking at a country's 'export basket', i.e. a list of the (main) products it exports, labelled with the percentage of total export revenue contributed by. Clothing and textiles form a large fraction of Bangladesh's export basket. For the US, in spite of the fact that its exports in these industries form a substantive fraction of world trade in clothing and textiles, the share of these goods in the US export basket is very small: these exports are crowded out in the US basket by a wide range of more technically advanced products. Clothing and textiles tend to carry a larger weight in the export baskets of poorer countries. Conversely, those countries for which pharmaceuticals carry a large weight in the export baskets tend to be relatively rich.

The underlying economics of this relationship is straightforward, but it requires a second key assumption. To see why, just begin from our idea of scarce capabilities, but now suppose that these scarce capabilities are scattered randomly across different countries: there might only be a handful of makers of large commercial jets, of heart-disease drugs, or of high-definition TVs. Yet if each country captures some slice of the scarcest capabilities, then we are back in a homogeneous world in which the derived demand for labour, and so wage rates

---

[1] This chapter is based on joint work with Daniel Trefler. The model set out in this chapter differs from that of Sutton and Trefler (2012) in two key respects: (i) it greatly simplifies the analysis by using a (strong and restrictive) 'small country' assumption, and (ii) instead of the conventional vertical labour supply schedule used in Sutton and Trefler (2012), it uses an upward sloping labour supply schedule. This is used in order to place the analysis in the same setting as is used in Chapter 3 below, where we look at the effects of changes in capability on both wages and employment.

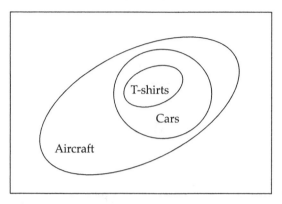

Fig. 2.1. Ranking Capabilities. Each oval corresponds to a country of a given 'type', and larger ovals indicate greater capabilities.

and GDP per capita, is the same in all countries. So to get to a link between a country's wealth and its production or export basket, we need a second key assumption: that the scarce capabilities are clustered geographically. The easiest version of this idea is one in which we rank the underlying capabilities, with the scarcest ones at the top. We can imagine this hierarchy of capabilities as a path along which countries advance. A country that has firms capable of producing aircraft certainly has firms capable of producing textiles. In other words, it's an 'inclusion' relationship. (Figure 2.1)

Now the notion that scarce capabilities are geographically clustered is self-evidently the case – and if we accept from this, the link from a country's wealth to its product and export mix follows. The question surrounding Assumption 2 is not whether it is the case – but rather, *why* it is the case. This is a deep question, and we set it on one side for the moment; and return to it in Section 2.7 below.

2.2. A SPECIAL SETTING

To keep things simple, let's begin by ranking industries and countries. The industries are ordered into groups running from the ones requiring the lowest level of capabilities (e.g. textiles) to those requiring the highest (e.g. aircraft). Now we'll rank the countries: a higher-ranked country can produce, at some standard level of productivity and quality, all the groups of goods that its lower-ranked counterpart can produce, and more besides, as in Figure 2.1. To simplify further, let's economize on labels and just say that a country of 'type k' is able to produce all products from product 1 to product k, but not higher-ranked products, $k + 1$, $k + 2$, etc. So the countries whose firms can produce products in group k are countries of type k, type $k + 1$, type $k + 2$, etc. To keep things simple, moreover, we'll assume that all firms in countries of type k, $k + 1$, $k + 2$, etc. have the same ('standard') level of productivity $1/c$ and quality u in the production of these goods.

In the model that follows, our first step will be to develop a setting that is familiar in the International Trade literature: a Ricardian model with complete specialization. The idea is this: country k has a wage level w_k that lies above the wage of the less capable group $k - 1$ countries, w_{k-1}. Thus the effective cost level of group k countries in the production of good $k - 1$ is higher than that of group $k - 1$ countries (i.e. it is $w_k c/u$ as against $w_{k-1} c/u$). If this gap is big enough, the k-type country will fail to meet the threshold for viability in the production of the $k - 1$ type goods. This, then, is the special setting of 'complete specialization': k-type countries make group k products, and only these products.

Under what conditions will this 'perfect sorting' outcome occur? Intuitively, we can see that this will depend on the values of n_k, the number of countries of type k. Suppose that, as we move to higher values of k, the number of k-type countries is (much) lower, i.e. there are much fewer $k + 1$ type countries than there are k type countries. Then the derived demand for labour in the production of group $k + 1$ goods will drive the equilibrium wage in $k + 1$ type countries to a level much higher than the wage in k type countries, thus ensuring that $k + 1$ type countries will be non-viable in the market for group k goods. This intuition underlies the condition for perfect sorting set out in the next section.

This, then, is the standard 'perfect sorting' setting that we construct as the backdrop to our analysis. Our analysis will focus on a 'small developing country' (the 'small' size of the country will mean we can neglect its impact on 'almost' all prices faced by consumers, and an international wage rate). Our small developing country will begin as a $k - 1$ type country: we will then allow it to begin producing group k products, initially at a low-quality level, which we will label v_k. This quality level will rise from zero, to the standard quality u offered by group k countries. We want to see what happens to its relative wage (our measure of its relative wealth), and its product mix, as this occurs.

2.3. THE MODEL

We begin with a formal restatement of the above description. All individuals in all countries have identical Cobb-Douglas utility functions defined over M goods, indexed by g, and labour:

$$U = \prod_g (u_g x_g)^{1/M} - \frac{1}{2} l^2 \qquad (2.1)$$

where l denotes hours of labour supplied, and u_g and x_g denote the quality and quantity of good g consumed. This is just an extension of the utility function of Section 1.13 to a setting with many goods. It has the familiar 'Cobb-Douglas' structure, and so the consumer spends the same fraction $1/M$ of income on each of the M goods, irrespective of their qualities and prices. A set of K countries, all with an equal population of workers[2] denoted **N**, are active in the production of M goods. The set of countries active in producing any specific good i at equilibrium depends on the value of the quality parameters and on equilibrium wage rates. We divide the K countries into T 'types', with n_k countries of type k so that $\sum_{k=1}^{k=T} n_k = K$. We divide the M goods into T equal-sized 'product groups', where m denotes the number of goods in each group, so $M = mT$.

We begin by describing a 'perfect sorting' case in which each country-type is associated at equilibrium with the production of exactly one 'product group'. With this in mind we set the number of country types equal to the number of product groups T. We further assume that all firms in countries of types $k, k + 1$, etc. who are capable of producing goods of group k, produce these goods at the same level of productivity and quality. We may then use the country index k to label, also, the set of goods produced at equilibrium by country k. In this setting, all producers of any good will operate in a country of

---

[2] As in Section 1.13, we assume there is a separate group of profit recipients who supply no labour, and have the same preferences over products.

the same type, and will face the same equilibrium wage level, and will produce the same output level of each good.

We assume there is (at most) one firm capable of producing any particular good, in each country, so that if a good is produced (only) by countries of type k, then the number of active producers of that good is n_k. We further assume that $n_k \geq 2$ for all k, so that there are at least two producers of every good.[3]

Countries in group k can produce all goods in product groups 1 to k at a 'standard' level of quality u, but not goods $k + 1$ and upward; the interpretation, as noted above, is that goods of a higher index require capabilities that are 'scarcer'. To get 'perfect sorting', it is sufficient to assume that $n_k \geq n_{k+1} + 4$ for all k. This ensures that goods in group k are produced, at equilibrium, only by countries of type k; and that all countries producing goods in this product group are of type k. The derivation of this result is straightforward, but lengthy, and since we need this merely as a backdrop to our main analysis, we relegate the derivation to Appendix 2.1.

2.4. A SMALL DEVELOPING COUNTRY

In this section, the aim is to examine a country initially producing good $k - 1$, whose capability in the production of good k improves, in the sense that its quality, denoted v_k, rises from zero to the standard quality u. (We set its productivity level equal to the standard level $1/c$ throughout.) As v_k rises, the country's mix of output will gradually shift from the production of goods of group $k - 1$ to goods of group k. This change will, in general, affect the equilibrium wage rate of all countries of adjacent types. The general solution in this setting is analytically intractable, and so we introduce a 'small' country approximation in order to permit a full solution. The idea is as follows: we begin from the benchmark model of the last section, but we now add in a new, additional, 'small' country whose initial capability level is low. This country's population is very small compared to the unit mass of workers in every other country. Moreover, its capabilities are confined to only the first η of the m products in each product group.

---

[3] If $n_k = 1$, the equilibrium (monopoly) price is undefined (i.e. goes to infinity); see equation (1.4).

The result will be that, when m is large, this country's presence (or absence) from the first η of the m markets of type k will have a negligible influence on the equilibrium wage of other (large) countries.[4] It will initially specialize in the production of $k - 1$ type goods, so the number of producers of the first η of the $k - 1$ type goods rises from n_{k-1} to $n_{k-1} + 1$. Hence, we may investigate the fortunes of this 'small developing country' while treating the wage rates of all other ('large') countries as being (approximately) constant.[5]

With this in mind, we proceed as follows. We begin from a situation in which the new country has the standard level of quality in the first η of the m products in each of the product groups 1 to $k - 1$; and has zero quality in all other products. Since the small country's equilibrium wage falls monotonically as its worker population rises, we can choose its worker population so that its equilibrium wage, when v_k reaches the level u, coincides with the equilibrium wage of type k countries. Once v_k reaches u, it will be active in, and only in, the first product of group k. Thus there are $n_k + 1$ producers in this market.

Phase I

We now examine the effect of allowing the small country's quality in the first η products of group k, which we denote by v_k, to rise from zero to the standard quality level u of existing group-k producers. This is illustrated in the left-hand curve in the top panel of Figure 2.2.

The rise in v_k has no effect on the new country's wage until v_k reaches the quality threshold at which the new country is viable in market k. This level of v_k, denoted v_k^c, is defined by the basic viability condition of Chapter 1 (equation (1.7′)), which in this setting takes the form[6]:

$$\frac{w(v_k^c)}{v_k^c} = \frac{n_k}{n_k - 1} \cdot \frac{w_k}{u}$$

---

[4] We need to assume η is large enough to justify treating firms in the small developing country as price takers in the labour market.

[5] We maintain here, as elsewhere, the assumption that the labour market faced by firms operating in country k is competitive, i.e. the firm is a price taker in the labour market.

[6] To see this, note that the effective cost level k_i becomes, in the present setting, $\frac{w_i c_i}{u_i}$; that c_i is the same for all firms, so that it cancels out; and that the number of rival firms, $n - 1$, becomes n_k in the present setting.

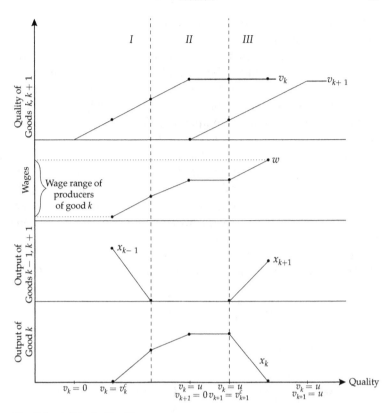

Fig. 2.2. A Rise in Quality

Notes: The top panel shows the new country's quality in good k advancing from $v_k = 0$ to $v_k = u$, and then its quality in good $k + 1$ advancing from $v_{k+1} = 0$ to $v_{k+1} = u$. The critical value of v_k at which production of good k becomes viable is labelled v_k^c, and is marked by the first dot on the v_k schedule. The second panel shows how the equilibrium wage rises as qualities rise, while the bottom two panels show how the output of goods $k - 1$, k, and $k + 1$ change. In the diagram, for ease of notation we have suppressed the subscripts and arguments of $w(v_k, v_{k+1})$, $x_{k-1}(w(v_k))$, $x_k(w(v_k, v_{k+1}), v_k, v_{k+1})$, and $x_{k+1}(w(v_{k+1}), v_{k+1})$.

where $w(v_k^c)$ is the small country's wage rate and w_k is the wage rate of group-k countries. v_k^c is shown on the horizontal axis of the bottom panel in Figure 2.2.

We have thus established the following key result. For $v_k \in (v_k^c, u)$ there will be a 'quality' range, that is, type-k products will be produced both at a low quality v_k by the small developing country, and also at the high 'standard' quality u by all type-k countries.

Once v_k advances beyond v_k^c, the new firm becomes active in both market $k - 1$ and market k; and this continues to be the case up to a critical level of v_k at which it ceases to be active in market $k - 1$. (This corresponds to the boundary between phases I and II in Figure 2.2.)

The central step in the analysis is to examine how the wage in the small developing country changes as v_k rises. The analysis rests on an examination of the country's output of goods $k - 1$ and good k, and so on the derived demand for labour in the country.

Its wage in phase I can be deduced as follows. Note that there are now $n_{k-1} + 1$ producers in market $k - 1$, all with quality u, where n_{k-1} producers have a local wage w_{k-1} and the small developing country has a local wage $w(v_k) > w_{k-1}$. There are $n_k + 1$ producers in market k, of which n_k have quality u and local wage w_k, while one has quality v_k and local wage $w(v_k)$.

We can now go to the basic 'output equation' of Chapter 1 (equation (1.5)), to write down the new country's output of a good of type $k - 1$:

$$x_{k-1} = \frac{1}{w(v_k)} S n_{k-1} \frac{w(v_k)/u}{n_{k-1}\frac{w_{k-1}}{u} + \frac{w(v_k)}{u}} \left\{ 1 - n_{k-1}\frac{w(v_k)/u}{n_{k-1}\frac{w_{k-1}}{u} + \frac{w(v_k)}{u}} \right\}$$

and its output of a good of type k is

$$x_k = \frac{1}{w(v_k)} S n_k \frac{w(v_k)/v_k}{n_k\frac{w_k}{u} + \frac{w(v_k)}{v_k}} \left\{ 1 - n_k\frac{w(v_k)/v_k}{n_k\frac{w_k}{u} + \frac{w(v_k)}{v_k}} \right\}$$

These expressions define a pair of functions $x_{k-1}(w(v_k))$ and $x_k(w(v_k), v_k)$ respectively. We note that x_{k-1} and x_k are monotonically decreasing in w (by property 1 of lemma 1, Chapter 1).

We now note that labour demand in the new country equals (recalling that the productivity parameters have been set to unity, and that it produces just the first η of the m goods of each type)

$$L^D = \eta x_{k-1}(w(v_k)) + \eta x_k(w(v_k), v_k)$$

while labour supply is

$$L^S = \lambda w(v_k)$$

where λ is a constant, independent of v_k, by our small country assumption. (This reflects the fact that consumers in this country, as in all other countries, face prices for goods, almost all of which are unchanged by the arrival of the small developing country.)

We measure the wage of the new country relative to the equilibrium wage of group-k countries. We have, on equating L^D to L^S,

$$\lambda w(v_k) = \eta x_{k-1}(w(v_k)) + \eta x_k(w(v_k), v_k) \qquad (2.2)$$

We begin by showing that, as v_k increases, w increases. To see this, differentiate (2.2) with respect to v_k to obtain

$$\lambda \frac{dw}{dv_k} = \eta \frac{\partial x_{k-1}}{\partial w} \cdot \frac{dw}{dv_k} + \eta \frac{\partial x_k}{\partial w} \cdot \frac{dw}{dv_k} + \eta \frac{\partial x_k}{\partial v_k}$$

whence

$$\frac{dw}{dv_k}[\lambda - \underbrace{\eta \frac{\partial x_{k-1}}{\partial w}}_{(-)} - \underbrace{\eta \frac{\partial x_k}{\partial w}}_{(-)}] = \underbrace{\eta \frac{\partial x_k}{\partial v_k}}_{(+)}$$

where the indicated signs on the derivatives follow from properties 1 and 2 of lemma 1. It follows that dw/dv_k is positive. In other words, the wage rate in the small developing country rises as its quality v_k rises. This is illustrated in the second panel of Figure 2.2.

To complete our analysis, we need a stronger result: we need to show that the wage rises *less than proportionally* with v_k, i.e. that $v_k/w(v_k)$ rises as v_k rises. To show this, suppose the contrary, namely that w rises proportionally more than v_k. By property 1 of lemma 1, this implies a fall in x_{k-1}. By properties 1 and 3 of lemma 1, this also implies a fall in x_k. Thus, the r.h.s. of (2.2) falls. However, the l.h.s. of (2.2) rises, which is a contradiction. It follows that, as v_k increases, w rises, but by a smaller proportional amount, so v_k/w rises.

These two results on the wage level lead to the implication for the small developing country's output of goods $k - 1$ and k.

Since w is rising, property 1 of lemma 1 implies that x_{k-1} falls. Since w is rising, but by less than v_k, properties 2 and 3 of lemma 1 imply that x_k rises. These results are illustrated in the two panels of Figure 2.2.

Phase II

This first phase, labelled phase I in Figure 2.2, ends when $w(v_k)$ rises to the critical value at which the new country is no longer viable in the production of goods of type $k - 1$. As v_k increases further, the new country specializes in the production of good k. Now labour market equilibrium requires

$$\lambda w(v_k) = x_k(w(v_k), v_k)$$

and $w(v_k)$ rises to w_k as v_k rises to u.[7]

It is worth noting that, in this phase, our new country produces exactly the same product mix as type-k countries, but is poorer, because of the lower quality of what it produces.

We note finally that, in Phase II, since w is rising, $x_k = \lambda w(v_k)$ must also be rising. This is shown in the bottom panel of Figure 2.2.

Phase III

We now extend the analysis by allowing our small developing country to build capabilities in the next group of products, i.e. in group $k + 1$. Specifically, we now denote by v_{k+1} the new country's quality level in the first product of group $k + 1$, holding its quality in products of group k at the standard quality level u. As before, there is no effect until its quality rises to a threshold level, corresponding to the boundary between phases II and III in Figure 2.2. Thereafter, following the same argument as set out above, its wage rises with v_{k+1} and output in market k now declines to zero as it becomes a 'high-quality' but 'high-wage' producer relative to incumbent firms (Phase III of Figure 2.2).

2.5. FROM THEORY TO EVIDENCE

The key prediction of the theory is that in general, equilibrium countries with different quality capabilities may nevertheless export the same good: at least some goods will be produced by a range of countries that have different levels of capabilities, and so different levels of GDP per capita.

This prediction is tested empirically in Sutton and Trefler (2012), to which the reader is referred for full details. Here, I remark on the main features of the evidence.

We begin from the idea of a country's 'export basket', i.e. the mix of its exports across different industries. Specifically, the export basket is described by giving the fraction of total exports accounted for by

---

[7] Differentiating this equation yields $\lambda \frac{dw}{dv_k} = \frac{\partial x_k}{\partial w} \frac{dw}{dv_k} + \frac{\partial x_k}{\partial v_k}$ or $\frac{dw}{dv_k} = [\lambda - \frac{\partial x_k}{\partial w}]^{-1}$ $\frac{\partial x_k}{\partial v_k}$. It follows from this, using properties 1 and 2 of lemma 1, that $\frac{dw_k}{dv_k} > 0$.

each industry, defined at the 4-digit ISIC level. To avoid 'noise' in the data, we take as a point of reference the industry accounting for the largest share in the basket, and we exclude from the basket all industries accounting for less than 1 per cent of the value of this 'leading' industry's exports.[8]

Once we have defined each country's export basket, we can then turn to analysing 'who exports what'. Our focus is on the *range* of countries that are exporters of each industry's products. We identify the 'poorest' and 'richest' exporter of each good: this corresponds to the end-points of the inverted-U curve in the bottom panel of Figure 2.2.

We then examine how, as we move from the poorest to the richest exporting country in this range, the weight of this industry's products in the country's export basket changes. This allows us to characterize empirically the 'inverted-U' relationship of Figure 2.2 (bottom panel).

One caveat is in order, however, which carries a cautionary message regarding the link between 'capabilities' and standard industry definitions. A 4-digit industry comprises, in most cases, a range of products that require higher or lower levels of manufacturing capabilities.[9] This means that the range of countries that are (significant) exporters of a given industry's products is in most cases very wide. This, in turn, means that drawing inferences about a country's industrial capabilities (or its wealth) from a description of its export basket, defined using standard industrial classification, is fraught with problems. This is discussed at length in Sutton and Trefler (2012); see also Appendix 2.2.

2.6. SUMMING UP: 'CAPABILITIES' REDEFINED

We defined a firm's capabilities in Chapter 1 as its quality and productivity levels for each narrowly defined submarket in which the firm may or may not operate. In this chapter, we have sharpened up

---

[8] This need to exclude 'noise' from trade data is a familiar problem in the literature. The value of 1 per cent need for the cut-off is arbitrary, but using a somewhat smaller or larger figure has no material effect on the results.

[9] It might be thought that moving to a lower level of aggregation might alleviate this problem, but this is not the case. The breakdown of industries at lower levels of aggregation does not, in most cases, distinguish between sub-industries requiring differing levels of manufacturing capabilities. For a discussion of this issue, see Sutton and Trefler (2012).

this definition by endogenizing the firm's decision to operate in some markets, and not to operate in others. (Though we have carried out the analysis by references to countries, rather than firms.)

So now we can label our central construct as a firm's, or a country's, *revealed* capability. What we can actually observe in the data (at best) is the set of markets in which a firm operates, and its quality and productivity in these markets. It is this observed *sub-set* of the pairs $(u, 1/c)$ that we label 'revealed capability'.

Beyond this conceptual advance, what we have pinned down in this chapter is a more refined version of the link between capabilities and wealth which we introduced at the end of Chapter 1 – we have, in so doing, offered a new way of looking at the much-studied relation between a country's wealth and the basket of goods that it exports.[10]

2.7. THE SECOND KEY ASSUMPTION REVISITED

The idea that capabilities are geographically clustered is the driving assumption of the literature on Geography and Trade that developed in the 1990s (Fujita, Krugman, and Venables 1999). Here, I want to cut directly to a key distinction between two kinds of story we can tell: distinguishing between these stories remains a deep and difficult problem. It is one of those issues that I identify in the final chapter as the major open question in relation to the present agenda.

There are two possible kinds of mechanism that may be involved. The first involves a flow of influence from one firm to another within each economy (solid arrows in Figure 2.3 (i)). This can come in various forms: firms can see what their local counterparts, partners, or rivals do, and emulate it. Individuals may leave one firm and join another, carrying know-how with them. Firms can contract to provide know-how along with capital equipment, then sell to local customers…and so on. That these influences operate more effectively across firms operating in the same country or region is arguable, though not compelling.

---

[10] This relation was first explored by Michaely (1984) and Lall, Weiss, and Zhang (2006), and has attracted widespread interest thanks to the work of Dani Rodrik, Ricardo Hausmann, and their several collaborators (see for example, Hausmann, Hwang, and Rodrik (2007)).

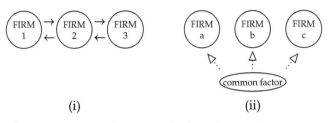

Fig. 2.3. Clustering of Capabilities

Another line of argument, shown in Figure 2.3 (ii), appeals to the presence of something outside the firms: a set of 'common factors' specific to each country that facilitate the formation of firms and their building up of capabilities. The list of putative common factors begins with institutions that provide education and training, legal and social institutions that enforce contracts and property rights and minimize corruption, and so on. If we follow this second route, then our present agenda of emphasizing the role of capabilities as the proximate cause of differences in national wealth becomes a rather weak programme. If it is only these more fundamental drivers that matter, any country that enjoys these fundamental drivers will see a flowering of firms developing ever-advancing capabilities. The transfer of capabilities across firms may be relatively unimportant.

These are deep issues, and we return to them in discussing the crucial role played by the transfer of capabilities across firms in Chapter 4.

3

Globalization I: The Shock of Liberalization

3.1. THE THIRD KEY ASSUMPTION: QUALITY VERSUS PRODUCTIVITY

Up to this point, the roles played by the 'demand shifter' of quality, u, and the 'cost shifter' of productivity, $1/c$, are closely similar. Indeed, the 'viability' condition of Chapter 1 (Equation (1.7)) implies that u and c matter only via the ratio u/c which appears in our 'effective cost' measure wc/u. But in this chapter, the point of departure is to introduce an assumption that will drive a wedge between the way 'quality' works, and the way 'productivity' works.

One of the most striking things I've noticed in conversations in Indian and Chinese firms these days is that productivity is rarely mentioned, while quality is a constantly recurring theme. (Box 3.1) Any deficiencies in productivity vis-à-vis international competition can be offset by low wages; yet even modest deficiencies in quality can make a product unsellable in world markets. It sounds obvious, but it doesn't fit with a story in which only the ratio effective cost measure wc/u matters to a firm's viability. What's missing here?

Before answering that question, let's look at a different way of motivating our examination of 'quality' versus 'productivity'. Over the past decade, a new literature has sprung up on 'Quality and Trade'. The driving force behind this literature lies in a simple empirical observation that emerged when trade economists first obtained access to large bodies of trade data at the level of the individual firm. Once they could look at each firm's export volume level alongside its price level, an interesting fact emerged: higher export prices went hand in hand with higher export volumes. Again, it seems obvious – until you ask about 'quality' versus 'productivity'. If the firms had the same quality levels, but differed in productivity, this would not be so. The higher productivity firms, with their lower cost levels, would have higher output and export volumes – but not higher prices.[1] Instead, we see high prices going hand in hand with high volumes, which is what happens when the difference between firms is based on quality: high-quality firms have both higher prices and higher sales. In other words, if you want to explain trade patterns at the firm level, you need to think in terms of the roles played by 'demand shifters'. What makes one firm more successful than another will involve both productivity and quality – but it seems that it's the quality differences that are dominant here: what makes exporting firms successful is in the first place driven by consumers' willingness-to-pay for whatever their product offers in comparison to those of rivals.

So why is quality different to productivity? Various answers can be suggested, but the one I want to advocate here (following Sutton (2007b)) has one great merit: it does not depend on the specifics of the technology used to produce a product, or on the nature of the customers to whom it is sold; it is equally valid for any manufactured good. It simply says: you can't make something out of nothing.

Manufacturing industry is concerned with transformation: the firm takes something in, whether raw material, semi-finished products, components and sub-assemblies, or whatever. It uses labour and capital to transform it into a sellable product – which might be sold either to final consumers, or to other firms. But the common denominator is that it starts from some material input – and that material input could as easily be sold to another firm, in another country. And once we have in place the idea that this material input commands some price on world markets, something fundamental follows.

Think of a world in which some countries have very low productivity, and also very low wages. In exporting products to world markets, their low wages offset their low productivity: it's only the unit wage cost, wc, that matters. Poor productivity in the form of a high value of c is offset by a corresponding low level of w. And this remains a valid point if we add in our 'cost of materials', so that your unit cost of production is no longer wc, but $wc + \mu p_0$, say, where μ is the quantity of material per unit of output, and p_0 is its (global) price. In a world of widget-makers, as we saw in Chapter 1, everyone can buy and sell

---

[1] In our present (Cournot) model, the prices of all firms' goods, being of the same quality, would have the same equilibrium price. In alternative models, such as a Bertrand model with horizontally differentiated products, these low-cost firms would have lower prices at equilibrium.

widgets at the same world price, and a country's level of w will simply adjust to compensate for poor productivity. A high value of c will lead to a low value of w: the country will be poor, but its firms will be just as viable as anyone else's.

But this argument fails in the case of quality. The unit cost of production is now $wc + \mu p_0$. Suppose some developing country has a low level of quality, v, while every other country has some higher quality u. Now if we stay with the Cournot model, prices vary in direct proportion with quality, so if the prevailing world price for the standard quality u is labelled p_u, then the price that the low-quality product v can command is lower than p_u, by the same ratio as the quality gap v/u. So the question is: can the developing country produce it at a cost low enough to sell it at this reduced price? Perhaps not. No matter how low the developing country's wage rate w falls, its unit cost of production $wc + \mu p_0$ cannot fall below μp_0. But that means that the lowest price at which the low quality product can be produced and sold must be at least equal to μp_0, no matter how low the developing country's wage. But to get customers to pay some price p_v, they have to be offered a price–quality ratio equal to that offered by other countries.

The implications of this can be explored by returning to the viability condition of Chapter 1 (Equation (1.7)), and replacing the expression for the marginal cost of production, wc, with $wc + \mu p_0$. If we label the (single) firm in the developing country as firm $n + 1$, and denote by $\bar{k}$ the mean of the effective cost levels of the existing n firms in the global market, then the threshold for viability is defined by

$$k_{n+1} = \frac{1}{n-1} \sum_{j=1}^{n} k_j = \frac{n}{n-1} \bar{k} \qquad (3.1)$$

Now suppose the firm in the developing country faces a 'local' wage rate (independent of the wage rates faced by existing producers in other countries), denoted by $\tilde{w}$.

Noting that $k_{n+1} = (\tilde{w} c_{n+1} + p_0 \mu)/u_{n+1}$, it follows that the schedule in $(1/c, u)$ space corresponding to Equation (3.1) takes the form of a right-angled hyperbola

$$u_{n+1} = \frac{1}{\bar{k}} \frac{n-1}{n} \left(\frac{\tilde{w}}{1/c_{n+1}} + \mu p_0 \right).$$

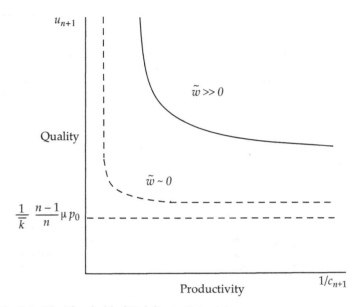

Fig. 3.1. The Threshold of Viability in $(1/c, u)$ Space

Notes: The wage at which firm $n + 1$ (alone) can hire labour is denoted by $\tilde{w}$. The dashed curve indicates the limiting form of the schedule as $\tilde{w} \to 0$.

This defines a threshold in $(u, 1/c)$ space, corresponding to the threshold shown in Chapter 1, Figure 1.2; it is illustrated in Figure 3.1. As $\tilde{w}$ falls to zero, the threshold in $(u, 1/c)$ space collapses inwards as shown in the Figure. On the horizontal (productivity) axis, it collapses to the vertical axis. On the vertical (quality) axis, it collapses to the horizontal line at

$$u = \frac{1}{\bar{k}} \frac{n-1}{n} \mu p_0.$$

If a firm has any $(v, 1/c)$ combination, such that v lies above this threshold, then we can find a local wage $\tilde{w}$ that is low enough to make our developing country's firm viable. But if v lies below this level, then the firm from the developing country cannot be viable, irrespective of how low the local wage falls.

This, then, is our point of departure: and it is the rediscovery of this result, and the following through of its implications, within a multi-country, general equilibrium setting, that forms the agenda of the present chapter.

Box 3.1. Quality versus Productivity

Machine tools are metal cutting machines, and they stand at the heart of the engineering sector. Today's machines are (computer) numerically controlled (CNC), and most machine tool makers buy the computer control unit for their machines from one of the world's two leading producers, Fanuc of Japan and Siemens of Germany.

The machines that concern me here are the Indian industry's leading product: CNC lathes of the most basic kind (known as 'single spindle, 2-axis' machines). In 2000 I benchmarked the production of Indian machines against equivalent machines imported from Taiwan. These imported machines had become the biggest sellers in the Indian market following the liberalization of trade that occurred during the 1990s. The question was, why?

The first half of my benchmarking exercise focussed on productivity and cost. It turned out that (labour) productivity was much higher in Taiwan: the number of labour-hours per machine for the average Taiwanese producer was one-sixth of that of the average Indian producer.[2] The wage rate, however, was eight times higher in Taiwan – so that the unit labour cost (the '*wc*' in the model of the text), was actually *lower* in India than in Taiwan.

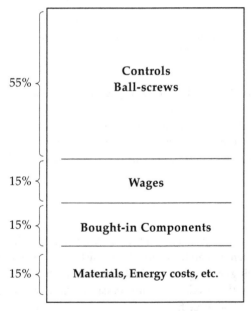

Fig. 3.2. Unit Costs for CNC Lathes in India

---

[2] The technique of production, and the degree of capital-intensity were similar in both countries.

What would happen if the Indian producers raised their productivity levels, reducing unit costs, and permitting a price cut? Figure 3.2 shows the cost breakdown for these machines: labour input accounts for only 15 per cent of unit cost (whereas the bought-in computer controls account for about half). A doubling of labour productivity would allow for only a fall of 7 or 8 per cent in price. Yet an examination of prices revealed that the Indian machines were selling for 25 per cent less than the Taiwanese.

The second half of the study was concerned with quality. By finding forty-nine factories in which a domestic Indian machine operated alongside an equivalent imported machine, cutting the same metal parts and supervised by the same production engineer, I could measure the quality difference between the two machines. This was a complex measurement exercise[3] which involved the production engineer completing a twenty-page questionnaire about all aspects of each machine – but the bottom line is quite simple. There was a very small quality difference, in favour of the imported machines. The single best summary measure is the recorded number of machine hours lost in the past year due to machine malfunction. The Indian machines were *slightly* worse, by about 3 per cent. Other aspects of quality revealed this same small but systematic gap; and this small quality difference was translating into a large price gap, and a serious loss of market share. (For more details on Indian machine tools, see Sutton (2001).)

[3] I am grateful to the Indian Machine Tool Manufacturers Association for their help with this.

3.2. THE GLOBALIZATION PROCESS: PHASE I

The process of globalization involves the liberalization of both trade flows, and capital movements. The first of these is the more heavily emphasized in discussions of the process, and it forms the subject of this section. The central theme of what follows, however, is that it is by no means the most important part of the process; quite the reverse.

There is a commonly told story regarding the effects of liberalizing trade between countries. It is one of economics' most central tales, but it needs to be told with care. The best way to begin is by thinking of two countries, between which no trade is initially possible, or permitted. When we switch to a regime of free trade, then both countries are better off. Why? Irrespective of what goods they initially produce, or what levels of productivity or quality their firms offer, trade can only improve matters. What trade does, is to bring about changes in the prices of traded goods, and this has effects on the sales volumes and employment levels of each firm. But all that's needed to ensure a welfare increase is that, for at least some pair of goods, *A* and *B*, the cost of the resources required to produce a unit of *A*, relative to the costs for a unit of *B*, differs between the two countries. This provides an opportunity for mutually advantageous trade: if one country finds it relatively more expensive to produce *A*, as compared to *B*, it should produce less *A* and more *B*, and use imports of *A* and exports of *B* to balance its domestic requirements. Now the beauty of this Ricardian argument from 'comparative advantage' is that it focuses only on the relative cost of producing *A* as opposed to *B*: the argument works even for a 'high capability' country trading with a 'low capability' country. The high capability country can produce both *A* and *B* using fewer labour hours than its counterpart, but so long as its cost of producing *A* compared to its cost of producing *B* differs from the relative cost of its potential trade partner, the argument goes through.

The collapse of the Soviet Union, and the resulting changes in political alignments in Eastern Europe, constitute one of the principle acts in the contemporary wave of globalization. Prior to 1989, Soviet bloc countries traded heavily among themselves; trade links to Western countries were extremely limited. Soviet raw materials flowed to Eastern Europe's manufacturers, at prices that reflected supply and demand, and various institutional rigidities, within the Soviet bloc. With the arrival of trade liberalization, this regime of partial trade gave just within a few years to a pretty liberal and open trading environment between East and West. With what results?

For economies in Eastern Europe, the early 1990s were a difficult period. Manufacturing capabilities, stunted by the absence of strong international competition for half a century, seriously lagged behind Western Europe. Trade liberalization led to factory closures and job losses as high-quality Western products drove low-price, low-quality local products off the market. But what of comparative advantage? Why did trade liberalization not lead to a good outcome?

The comparative advantage example I offered above was designed to exclude one key consideration. By starting with just two countries, and supposing there was no trade to begin with, we miss one vital consideration. Start instead from a world with many countries. Imagine that, to begin with, some products and commodities are traded between some countries, but for other commodities and countries, trade is prohibited. Now move from this 'partial trade' setting to a completely open global trading regime. In this setting, it is no longer the case that trade liberalization necessarily helps all countries. To see what can happen, think of the infamous Trabants that drove through the Berlin Wall in November 1989. During the Soviet era, Russian steel could be imported profitably by East Germany to make Trabant engines. Post liberalization, there was a world market in which Soviet steel could find a higher price. Meanwhile, East Germany's consumers could buy higher-quality Volkswagens at higher prices than Trabants; and they did so. The price of steel, imported at world prices, made it unprofitable to make Trabant engines, given the price these could command on world markets. Another way of looking at this is to say that, from a global efficiency point of view, it was a poor use of resources to turn Soviet steel into low-quality Trabant engines, when it could just as easily be transformed by a more capable firm into a Volkswagen engine – and the new regime of prices for materials and final products that emerged in the world of the early 1990s was ensuring that this inefficient use of resources was eliminated.

Which was bad news for eastern Germany: the derived demand for labour fell along with the fall in demand for Trabant engines. And here, at last, we come full circle to the 'materials cost' with which we began. Once again, we ask: if labour demand was falling in Eastern Europe, then why would a resulting fall in wages not restore the viability of firms and ensure that employment levels were protected? The answer lies in the 'materials cost' idea: given the low quality of the final goods produced, no matter how great the fall in wages, these goods would not become viable – the floor to price set by the cost of the material inputs required in their manufacture doomed them to failure.

The result, throughout the Eastern bloc, was a mix of job losses, firm failures, and expensive government programme of job protection and firm subsidies. Different countries used a different package of measures; and the consequent impact on employment, and firm profitability varied accordingly. But the overall impact was negative. The first phase of globalization, which had for many areas of the world proved hugely beneficial, did not do any favours for Eastern Europe.[4]

---

[4] As Roland and Verdier (1999) note, the economics of Eastern Europe suffered an output fall that 'was contemporaneous with price and trade liberalization'. They remark that this output fall is 'very difficult to explain ... with standard macroeconomic analysis alone', and they propose an explanation based on the time needed for firms to establish new business networks within the liberalized economy. The present analysis offers an alternative candidate explanation, which fits with the fact that recovery coincided with an inflow of Foreign Direct Investment. (For other views on this issue, see Gomulka (1991), Winiecki (1991), Kiguel and Liviatan (1992), Kornai (1993), and Aslund (1994).)

But the second phase, as we will see in the next chapter, was a very different story.

3.3. THE MODEL

As in Chapter 2, we assume that all individuals in all countries share the same utility function defined over M goods, and labour,

$$U = \prod_{g=1}^{M} (u_g x_g)^{1/M} - \frac{1}{2} l^2 \tag{3.2}$$

and we assume a separate group of profit recipients whose utility function is the same as this, but who do not supply labour ($l \equiv 0$).

It follows from examining the workers' constrained optimization problem (as in Chapter 1, Section 1.13) that individual labour supply takes the form[5]

$$l = \frac{w}{M} \prod_{g=1}^{M} \left(\frac{u_g}{p_g}\right)^{1/M} \tag{3.3}$$

so that labour supply is directly proportional to the wage w.

Substituting this into the utility function (3.2) we have for the individual's utility,

$$U = \frac{1}{2} \left(\frac{w}{M}\right)^2 \prod_{g=1}^{M} \left(\frac{u_g}{p_g}\right)^{2/M} \tag{3.4}$$

There are three countries, each with a population of **N** workers. Countries A and B can produce all M 'final' goods, while C produces raw material.

---

[5] The Cobb–Douglas form in (3.2) implies that the consumer spends fraction $1/M$ of income wl on each of the M goods, so $p_g x_g = wl/M$ for all g, whence

$$x_g = \frac{1}{M} \cdot \frac{wl}{p_g}$$

Substituting this for x_g in (3.2) to obtain

$$U = \frac{w}{M} \prod_g \left(\frac{u_g}{p_g}\right)^{1/M} \cdot l - \frac{1}{2} l^2$$

and setting $\frac{dU}{dl} = 0$ we obtain (3.3).

In the preceding chapter, we divided all goods into groups, corresponding to different levels of manufacturing capability required for their production. In this chapter, we have just two groups of (final) goods. The first group, indexed $1, \ldots, r$ are 'commodity type' products, for which countries A and B have the same level of capability, i.e. productivity and quality are the same for all firms in both countries.

I label their quality as 1 and the number of units of labour required per unit of output as c_1. I assume the number of (potential) producers of each of these goods is the same in both countries, and denote this number by n_1. My focus of interest will lie in the case where n_1 is large.[6]

The remaining group of products, indexed $r + 1, r + 2, \ldots, M$, require a higher level of capability. Here, firms in country B have a lower level of capability than those in country A.

I denote by u the (common) quality level attained by all firms in country A in the production of goods $r + 1$ to M; and by c_A the (common) number of labour units needed per unit of output. The corresponding quality and productivity parameters for country B are denoted by v and c_B. I denote by n the number of (potential[7]) producers of each of these goods, in each country.

I will assume as before that the number of industries M is fixed and is 'large'.[8] My main focus of interest will lie in the case where most goods are 'quality' goods, i.e. r/M is small.

The production of a unit of any of these goods requires μ units of an (internationally traded) raw material for each unit of final good produced. This raw material is supplied from country C. I assume that the number of producers of this intermediate good in country C is large and each of these firms can produce one unit of raw material using one unit of labour input; at equilibrium, this will imply that the price of the raw material input equals the wage rate in country C.

---

[6] This can be motivated by supposing the effectiveness of R&D spending in raising capability to be low in these industries – the 'exogenous sunk cost' limit; see Sutton (2007a).

[7] Some of these firms may be inactive at equilibrium.

[8] This allows me, as before, to treat firms as price takers in labour markets and to assume that each firm takes total consumer demand as fixed when choosing its output level.

3.4. THE PRE-GLOBALIZATION EQUILIBRIUM

We begin with a pre-globalization world. The raw material supplying country C is partitioned into two equal parts, each with population $N/2$, labelled 'East' and 'West'. The raw material supplies of Western C supply country A, and those of Eastern C supply country B; no trade of raw materials or final products or migration of workers is permitted between the Eastern Bloc and Western Bloc countries.

In what follows, we examine the equilibrium outcome in the Western bloc, A plus Western C. (The analysis carries over to the Eastern bloc, via a simple relabelling of parameters.)

The analysis that follows will lead us to expressions for the utility of a worker in each country. The analysis, and the results, for country A, are similar to those set out for a single economy in the final part of Chapter 1 (Section 1.13). The difference lies in the role played by A's raw materials input from country C.

Note first that the unit cost of goods $1, \ldots, r$ in country A is $w_A c_1 + w_C \mu$, where w_C denotes the wage in the 'region' of C attached to the A market. Similarly the unit cost of production of goods $r + 1, \ldots, M$ is $w_A c_A + w_C \mu$. It follows on substituting for the effective cost parameters in the basic output equation (Chapter 1, Equation (1.5)), and noting that expenditure on industry i's products equals S/M, that equilibrium prices p_1 and quantities x_1 (for goods $1, \ldots, r$) and p_u and x_u (for goods $r + 1, \ldots, M$) satisfy

$$p_u = \frac{n}{n-1}(w_A c_A + w_C \mu); \quad p_1 = \frac{n_1}{n_1 - 1}(w_A c_1 + w_C \mu) \qquad (3.5)$$

$$x_u = \frac{S}{M} \frac{n-1}{n^2} \frac{1}{w_A c_A + w_C \mu}; \quad x_1 = \frac{S}{M} \frac{n_1 - 1}{n_1^2} \frac{1}{w_A c_1 + w_C \mu} \qquad (3.6)$$

Substituting (3.5) into (3.4), and writing the expression

$$\left[\frac{(n-1)}{n}\right]^{2(M-r)/M} \left[\frac{(n_1 - 1)}{n_1}\right]^{2r/M}$$

as $\mathbb{N}$ to ease notation, gives

$$U_A = \frac{1}{2}\left(\frac{w_A}{M}\right)^2 \mathbb{N}\left(\frac{u}{w_A c_A + w_C \mu}\right)^{2(M-r)/M} \left(\frac{1}{w_A c_1 + w_C \mu}\right)^{2r/M} \qquad (3.7)$$

Equilibrium in the labour market can be analysed as follows: Since each unit of final good produced in A requires μ units of material (and so μ units of labour from C) and either c_1 or c_A units of labour from A (for goods $1, \ldots, r$ and $r + 1, \ldots, M$ respectively), it follows that labour demand satisfies

$$L_C^D = (M - r)n\mu x_u + rn_1\mu x_1$$

$$L_A^D = (M - r)nc_A x_u + rn_1 c_1 x_1$$

From the individual labour supply function (3.3),

$$L_A^S = Nl_A^s = N\frac{w_A}{M}\left(\frac{u}{p_u}\right)^{\frac{M-r}{M}}\left(\frac{1}{p_1}\right)^{\frac{r}{M}}$$

$$L_C^S = \frac{1}{2}Nl_C^s = \frac{1}{2}N\frac{w_C}{M}\left(\frac{u}{p_u}\right)^{\frac{M-r}{M}}\left(\frac{1}{p_1}\right)^{\frac{r}{M}}$$

The four equations in (3.5) and (3.6), together with the labour market clearing conditions $L_A^S = L_A^D$ and $L_C^S = L_C^D$, determine the unknowns $p_u, p_1, w_A, w_C, x_u, x_1$, and S up to a numeraire.[9]

The relation between w_C and w_A is as follows: from the form of the labour supply functions (3.3) above, it follows that the ratio of labour supply in the first region of country C (whose population is $N/2$), and which we denote by L_C^S, to labour supply in country A, L_A^S satisfies

$$\frac{L_C^S}{L_A^S} = \frac{1}{2}\frac{w_C}{w_A} \tag{3.8}$$

while the labour demand functions imply

$$\frac{L_C^D}{L_A^D} = \frac{(M - r)n\mu x_u + rn_1\mu x_1}{(M - r)nc_A x_u + rn_1 c_1 x_1} \tag{3.9}$$

Equating (3.8) and (3.9), we have for the special case of interest in which $r \to 0$ that

$$\frac{w_C}{w_A} = 2\frac{\mu}{c_A}$$

---

[9] In other words, the *nominal* price level is not determined, but the prices and wages are fixed relative to S. S represents total expenditure on final goods and can be written as

$$(M - r)np_u x_u + rn_1 p_1 x_1.$$

and so from (3.7), we have

$$U_A = \frac{\mathbb{N}}{2M^2}\left(\frac{u}{c_A + 2\mu^2/c_A}\right)^2. \text{ Similarly, } U_B = \frac{\mathbb{N}}{2M^2}\left(\frac{v}{c_B + 2\mu^2/c_B}\right)^2$$

(3.10)

These expressions can be compared to the equivalent expressions in Section 1.13. When $M = 1$ and $\mu = 0$, the expressions are identical.

3.5. TRADE LIBERALIZATION: REGIME I

We now examine Phase I of the globalization process, by opening up free trade between A and B, while abolishing the partition between the two parts of country C. We will see in what follows that, depending on the size of the gap in capabilities between A and B, there are three possible regimes. We begin with the case where the gap is small. In this case, as we will see, all goods are produced in both A and B.

There are no 'trade costs', or 'costs of transport'. Each (final) good is now sold in a single 'international' market, and since each of goods 1 to r is sold by $2n_1$ firms, and each of goods $r + 1$ to M is sold by $2n$ firms, and all goods incur a unit materials cost of $w_C\mu$, it follows from the basic price equation (1.4), and replacing S by S/M as before, that when all firms are active at equilibrium, the (quality-adjusted) prices of each quality good $r + 1$ to M satisfy

$$\frac{p_u}{u} = \frac{p_v}{v} = \frac{n}{2n-1}\left(\frac{w_A c_A + w_C\mu}{u} + \frac{w_B c_B + w_C\mu}{v}\right) \quad (3.11)$$

while the prices of each commodity good 1 to r are equal to

$$p_1 = \frac{n_1}{2n_1 - 1}[(w_A c_1 + w_C\mu) + (w_B c_1 + w_C\mu)]. \quad (3.12)$$

The corresponding (quality-adjusted) outputs for the quality goods are:

$$u x_u = \frac{S}{M} \times \frac{2n-1}{n} \times \frac{1}{\left(\frac{w_A c_A + w_C\mu}{u} + \frac{w_B c_B + w_C\mu}{v}\right)}$$

$$\times \left[1 - \frac{2n-1}{n} \times \frac{w_A c_A + w_C\mu}{u\left(\frac{w_A c_A + w_C\mu}{u} + \frac{w_B c_B + w_C\mu}{v}\right)}\right] \quad (3.13)$$

$$vx_v = \frac{S}{M} \times \frac{2n-1}{n} \times \frac{1}{\left(\frac{w_A c_A + w_C \mu}{u} + \frac{w_B c_B + w_C \mu}{v}\right)}$$

$$\times \left[1 - \frac{2n-1}{n} \times \frac{w_B c_B + w_C \mu}{v\left(\frac{w_A c_A + w_C \mu}{u} + \frac{w_B c_B + w_C \mu}{v}\right)}\right] \quad (3.14)$$

so long as the term in $[\cdot]$ on the r.h.s. expression is positive, in each case, and zero otherwise. (In the latter case, the corresponding firms are inactive at equilibrium.) The output of each commodity good 1 produced in country A is

$$x_{1A} = \frac{S}{M} \times \frac{2n_1 - 1}{n_1} \times \frac{1}{(w_A c_1 + w_C \mu) + (w_B c_1 + w_C \mu)}$$

$$\times \left[1 - \frac{2n_1 - 1}{n_1} \frac{w_A c_1 + w_C \mu}{(w_A c_1 + w_C \mu) + (w_B c_1 + w_C \mu)}\right]$$

while in country B it is

$$x_{1B} = \frac{S}{M} \times \frac{2n_1 - 1}{n_1} \times \frac{1}{(w_A c_1 + w_C \mu) + (w_B c_1 + w_C \mu)}$$

$$\times \left[1 - \frac{2n_1 - 1}{n_1} \frac{w_B c_1 + w_C \mu}{(w_A c_1 + w_C \mu) + (w_B c_1 + w_C \mu)}\right] \quad (3.15)$$

so long as the term in $[\cdot]$ on the r.h.s. expression is positive, and zero otherwise.

Finally, note that under liberalization, consumers in all countries face the same quality–price ratios, so that labour supply satisfies

$$L_A^S = N\frac{w_A}{M} \prod_i \left(\frac{u_i}{p_i}\right)^{1/M}, L_B^S = N\frac{w_B}{M} \prod_i \left(\frac{u_i}{p_i}\right)^{1/M},$$

$$L_C^S = N\frac{w_C}{M} \prod_i \left(\frac{u_i}{p_i}\right)^{1/M}$$

whence L_A^S, L_B^S, and L_C^S stand in the same ratio as w_A, w_B, and w_C, namely

$$L_A^S : L_B^S : L_C^S = w_A : w_B : w_C$$

I begin by remarking on the fully symmetric case, where $u = v$ and $c_A = c_B$. Note that in this case the expression in $[\cdot]$ in (3.13),

(3.14), and (3.15) reduces to $1/(2n)$ and $1/(2n_1)$ respectively. To ease notation, write

$$\left[\frac{(2n-1)}{2n}\right]^{2(M-r)/M}\left[\frac{(2n_1-1)}{2n_1}\right]^{2r/M}$$

as $\mathbb{N}'$. I focus, as before, on the limiting case where $r=0$. Since each unit of output in A or B requires $c_A (= c_B)$ units of local labour and μ units of materials, we have

$$L_C^D = 2(\mu/c_A)L_A^D = 2(\mu/c_B)L_B^D$$

whence $w_C = 2(\mu/c_A)w_A = 2(\mu/c_B)w_B$ and our expressions for the unit cost of production (marginal cost) become:

$$w_A c_A + w_C\mu = w_B c_B + w_C\mu = w_A\left(c_A + 2\frac{\mu^2}{c_A}\right).$$

It follows from (3.4) and (3.11) that, in the limiting case

$$r = 0,$$

following the same argument as before, that in this setting where $u = v$ we have

$$U_A = \frac{\mathbb{N}'}{2M^2}\left(\frac{u}{c_A + 2\mu^2/c_A}\right)^2 = \frac{\mathbb{N}'}{2M^2}\left(\frac{v}{c_B + 2\mu^2/c_B}\right)^2 = U_B \quad (3.16)$$

The only difference with the pre-globalization case lies in the terms $\mathbb{N}' > \mathbb{N}$; this reflects the fact that there are now twice as many producers competing in the market for each good, so that prices fall, and our welfare measure rises. This 'price' effect is analogous to the effect of liberalization in the standard Dixit–Stiglitz–Krugman CES framework; but an important difference is that, in the present setting, all fixed costs are sunk, and liberalization does not induce exit, but leads to a fall in profits. This comment notwithstanding, this first regime, then, in which capabilities are closely similar in countries A and B, will look very familiar to readers acquainted with the standard Dixit–Stiglitz–Krugman type models of intra-industry trade. It is when we turn in the next section to Regime II, where capability differences are greater, that the central ideas of the present analysis begin to appear.

3.6. TRADE LIBERALIZATION: REGIME *II*

As v falls below u, the wage in B falls below the wage in A. For the commodity type goods, the quality remains the same, however. There is a critical level of v at which the wage in B falls to the point where A is no longer viable in the production of commodity goods, and these goods are produced only by B. On the assumption that n_1 is 'large', a correspondingly small difference in wage rates suffices to render A's production of commodity goods unviable. Once v falls below the critical level, we enter Regime *II*, where A and B both produce quality goods, but B is the sole producer of the commodity goods.

The (quality-adjusted) prices of goods $r + 1$ to M are now given by (3.11) and the quality-adjusted outputs are given by (3.13), (3.14). For the commodity good, however, $x_{1A} = 0$ and, noting that only a total of n_1 producers (those in B) now operate, it follows that[10]

$$x_{1B} = \frac{S}{M} \frac{n_1 - 1}{n_1^2} \frac{1}{w_B c_1 + w_C \mu} \tag{3.17}$$

The key question of interest relates to the viability of the (low) quality goods produced in country B. This threshold is defined by setting the expression in [·] in the output equation for v, Equation (3.14), to zero. Before examining this, however, we complete our description of the three regimes, by examining the third regime, in which v has fallen to a level at which B's quality goods are no longer viable. In this regime, A is the sole producer of quality goods and B is the sole producer of commodity goods.

3.7. TRADE LIBERALIZATION: REGIME *III*

In Regime *III*, the equation describing the quality-adjusted output of products $r + 1$ to M in country B ((3.14) above) collapses to $v x_v = 0$. Since each of the goods $r + 1, \ldots, M$ is produced only by its n producers in country A, we have from the basic price and output equations (1.4) and (1.5) that

---

[10] This equation may be derived from a limit case of the Regime *I* equations as follows: set the (bracketed term in the) expression x_{1A} in (3.15) to zero, to obtain the criterion $(w_A c_1 + w_C \mu)/(w_B c_1 + w_C \mu) = n_1/(n_1 - 1)$. Substitute this into the expression for x_{1B} to obtain (3.17).

$$p_u = \frac{n}{n-1}(w_A c_A + w_C \mu) \tag{3.18}$$

$$x_u = \frac{S}{M} \frac{n-1}{n^2} \frac{1}{w_A c_A + w_C \mu} \tag{3.19}$$

which replace (3.11) and (3.13) above. Products 1 to r are produced in country B only, whence their prices and outputs equal

$$p_1 = \frac{n_1}{n_1 - 1}(w_B c_1 + w_C \mu) \tag{3.20}$$

$$x_{1B} = \frac{S}{M} \frac{n_1 - 1}{n_1^2} \frac{1}{w_B c_1 + w_C \mu} \tag{3.21}$$

as in (3.17) above.

The labour supply equations, following the same argument as before, imply in this regime that

$$\frac{L_A^S}{L_B^S} = \frac{w_A}{w_B} = \frac{L_A^D}{L_B^D} = \frac{M - r}{r} \frac{c_A}{c_1} \frac{n x_u}{n_1 x_{1B}} \tag{3.22}$$

which on substituting for x_u, x_1 from (3.19), (3.21) implies,

$$\frac{w_A}{w_B} = \frac{M - r}{r} \frac{c_A}{c_1} \frac{n-1}{n} \frac{n_1}{n_1 - 1} \frac{(w_B c_1 + w_C \mu)}{(w_A c_A + w_C \mu)} \tag{3.23}$$

Since each unit of output in A requires c_A units of local labour and μ units of materials, and each unit of output in B requires c_1 units of labour and μ units of materials, and since each unit of materials requires one unit of labour in country C, we have

$$L_C^D = \mu \left(\frac{1}{c_A} L_A^D + \frac{1}{c_1} L_B^D \right)$$

and since

$$L_A^D : L_B^D : L_C^D = L_A^S : L_B^S : L_C^S = w_A : w_B : w_C, \tag{3.24}$$

it follows that

$$w_C = \mu \left(\frac{w_A}{c_A} + \frac{w_B}{c_1} \right) \tag{3.25}$$

Using (3.25) to substitute for w_C in (3.23), rearranging, writing the wage ratio w_B/w_A as ω, and letting $n_1 \to \infty$, gives

$$\frac{1}{\omega} = \frac{M - r}{r} \frac{n-1}{n} \frac{c_A}{c_1} \frac{\mu^2/c_A + \omega(c_1 + \mu^2/c_1)}{(c_A + \mu^2/c_A) + \omega \mu^2/c_1}$$

Now our focus of interest lies in showing that as the number of commodity goods, r, becomes small, the wage in country B, which produces only these goods, becomes arbitrarily low in comparison to the wage in A. In other words, we want to establish that, in the limit $r \to 0$, we have $\omega = w_B/w_A \to 0$. To see this, note that the preceding equation can be rearranged to give a quadratic equation in ω, as follows:

$$\left(c_1 + \frac{\mu^2}{c_1} \right) \omega^2 + \frac{\mu^2}{c_A} \left(1 - \frac{r}{M - r\,n - 1}\,\frac{n}{} \right) \omega$$

$$- \frac{r}{M - r\,n - 1}\,\frac{n}{}\,c_1 \left(1 + \frac{\mu^2}{c_A^2} \right) = 0 \qquad (3.26)$$

Our focus of interest lies in the case where r/M is small. Recall that $n \geq 2$ and note that the second coefficient is therefore positive for $r/M < 3$; and that the first and third coefficients are positive and negative respectively. The value of the wage ratio ω is defined by the (single) positive root. (See Figure 3.3.) The third coefficient, and so the value of $\omega = w_B/w_A$, falls to zero in the limiting case where $r = 0$. This property will be used in examining welfare effects in what follows (Section 3.9).

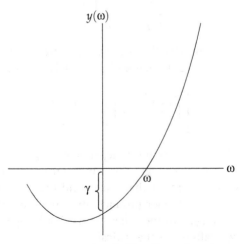

Fig. 3.3. Illustrating Equation (3.26). The illustration shows the quadratic function $y(\omega) = \alpha\omega^2 + \beta\omega - \gamma$ with $\alpha, \beta, \gamma > 0$. The solution to (3.26) is given by the positive root, labelled w^* in the figure.

3.8. QUALITY VERSUS PRODUCTIVITY

I now turn to the critical values of v and c_B which, for given values of u and c_A, correspond to the boundary between zones II and III at which country B's production of the 'quality' goods $r + 1, \ldots, M$ becomes non-viable. A necessary and sufficient condition for $x_v > 0$ is obtained by setting the expression in $[\cdot]$ in equation (3.14) to zero, and rearranging:

$$\frac{w_A c_A + w_C \mu}{w_B c_B + w_C \mu} \frac{v}{u} > \frac{n-1}{n} \tag{3.27}$$

Writing $w_C = \mu(w_A/c_A + w_B/c_1)$, this becomes

$$\frac{w_A c_A + \mu^2 \left(\frac{w_A}{c_A} + \frac{w_B}{c_1}\right)}{w_B c_B + \mu^2 \left(\frac{w_A}{c_A} + \frac{w_B}{c_1}\right)} \frac{v}{u} > \frac{n-1}{n} \tag{3.28}$$

It is important to note the asymmetry between the quality parameters (u, v) and the productivity parameters (c_A, c_B) in (3.28); and to note that this asymmetry disappears in the special case $\mu = 0$, when (3.28) can be expressed as a condition on the capability ratio, namely

$$\frac{v}{u} \frac{c_A}{c_B} > \frac{n-1}{n} \frac{w_B}{w_A} \tag{3.29}$$

To explore the asymmetry that arises in the case $\mu > 0$, we consider the limiting case of (3.28) when $w_B/w_A \to 0$. Here, (3.28) reduces to

$$\left[\left(\frac{c_A}{\mu}\right)^2 + 1\right] \frac{v}{u} > \frac{n-1}{n} \tag{3.30}$$

Note that the l.h.s. expression is independent of c_B; if $v = u$, then for any value of c_B, however high, this condition is satisfied (the l.h.s. expression is strictly greater than unity, and the r.h.s. expression is strictly less than unity). Poor productivity can always be offset by a sufficiently low wage. On the other hand, (3.30) implies that if the quality ratio v/u falls below the critical level

$$\left.\frac{v}{u}\right|_{crit} = \frac{n-1}{n} \frac{1}{1 + (c_A/\mu)^2} \tag{3.31}$$

then v is non-viable even if the wage ratio w_B/w_A falls to zero. This is the analogue in the present general equilibrium setting of the 'quality window' property illustrated in Figure 3.1.[11]

3.9. WELFARE

We now compare the welfare of country B, as measured by U_B, as a function of its quality v, under Pre-Globalization and under Trade Liberalization (Figure 3.4). Note that, under Pre-Globalization, U_B falls with v, and when $r = 0$, as $v \to 0$, $U_B \to 0$. (Equation (3.10)). Under Liberalization, U_B falls with v until v falls to a critical level below which B no longer produces the quality good, i.e. we move from Regime II to Regime III. When v is below this level, U_B is independent of v, i.e. the U_B schedule becomes flat. In this section, we examine the properties of the U_B schedule under Liberalization, as illustrated in Figure 3.4. I begin by looking at Regime III. Here, using the general expression (3.4) for the welfare indicator gives

$$U_B = \frac{1}{2} \left(\frac{w_B}{M} \right)^2 \mathbb{N} \left(\frac{u}{w_A c_A + w_C \mu} \right)^{2(M-r)/M} \left(\frac{1}{w_B c_1 + w_C \mu} \right)^{2r/M} \tag{3.32}$$

which on using (3.25) to write $w_C = \mu(w_A/c_A + w_B/c_1)$ becomes

$$\frac{\mathbb{N}}{2M^2} \left(\frac{w_B}{w_A} \right)^2 \left[\frac{u}{c_A + \mu^2 (\frac{1}{c_A} + \frac{w_B}{w_A} \frac{1}{c_1})} \right]^{2(M-r)/M} \left[\frac{1}{\frac{w_B}{w_A} c_1 + \mu^2 (\frac{1}{c_A} + \frac{w_B}{w_A} \frac{1}{c_1})} \right]^{2r/M} \tag{3.33}$$

We are now in a position to establish the key relationship between welfare in the 'Liberalization' world, and that of the 'Pre-globalization' world, as illustrated in Figure 3.4. In the Figure, the point of interest is that the Liberalization curve will, for small r, lie below that of the Pre-globalization curve for some intermediate range of v. To establish this property, we show that the point labelled X in Figure 3.4, which marks the boundary between Regime II and Regime III, must always lie to the right of the critical value of v; and that as $r \to 0$ it must fall down onto the horizontal axis. From this it follows that the

---

[11] The ratio $1/[1 + (c_A/\mu)^2]$ in (3.31) represents the most favourable unit cost ratio that B can enjoy in producing v, relative to A in producing u. To see this, note that B's unit cost cannot fall below $\mu w_C = (\mu^2/c_A)w_A$ while A's unit cost is $w_A c_A + w_C \mu = (c_A + \mu^2/c_A)w_A$.

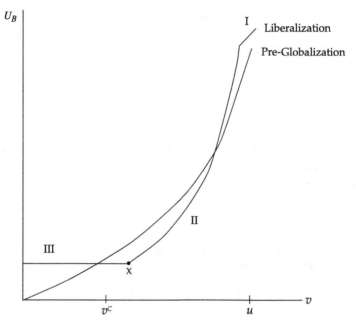

Fig. 3.4. The Welfare Indicator U_B as a Function of B's Relative Quality under Liberalization versus Pre-Globalization

Notes: The label v^c indicates the value of v at which the quality ratio $\frac{v}{u}$ lies at the critical level defined by equation (3.31).

post-liberalization curve must cross the (quadratic) pre-globalization schedule. Specifically, we proceed in three steps, as follows:

(i) We first focus on the critical value of v, defined (relative to u) by (3.31). We label this value as v^C in Figure 3.4. We note from (3.10) that the value of U_B in the Pre-globalization case is strictly positive at this (strictly positive) value of v, in the limiting case of interest, i.e. where $r \to 0$, as illustrated in Figure 3.4.

(ii) We now note that the range of v corresponding to Regime III extends from zero to some point above v^C (in Figure 3.4, this range extends to the point labelled X).[12] For $v < v^C$, the $U_B(v)$ schedule is

---

[12] To see why the critical value lies *above* v^C, recall that $\left.\frac{v}{u}\right|_{crit}$ is defined in (3.31) by reference to the limiting case $r \to 0$, where w_B/w_A falls to zero in Regime III. With a (small) positive value of r, w_B/w_A is positive in Regime III, and the critical level of v at which B becomes non-viable in the production of quality goods is strictly higher than v^C.

flat, as further falls in v below v^C have no effect on U_B. So the value of U_B in Regime III is constant. In particular, the value of U_B at $v = v^C$ in the Liberalization case equals the (constant) value of U_B in Regime III, as given by Equation (3.33). (Figure 3.4 shows the Liberalization schedule for small positive r).

(iii) We now show that this flat portion of the $U_B(v)$ schedule, corresponding to the value of U_B in Regime III, as given by (3.33), falls to the horizontal axis as $r \rightarrow 0$. To see this, recall that we showed in the final step of Section 3.7 that, in the limit $r \rightarrow 0$, we have $w_B/w_A \rightarrow 0$, whence it follows from expression (3.33) that $U_B \rightarrow 0$.

It follows that for sufficiently low values of r, the Liberalization schedule lies below the Pre-globalization schedule over some part of its range (around the point X). So in this zone, the move from the 'partial trade' setting of Pre-globalization to full liberalization reduces U_B.

The relevant point of reference in traditional trade theory is as follows: within a three- (or more) country model, a move from partial restrictions on trade to full liberalization is not necessarily welfare improving for all countries: the outcome depends on movements in the terms of trade.

The intuition is as follows: if v is close to zero, the economy's pre-globalization level of activity, and welfare, is very low, and the benefit of gaining access to u outweighs the effects on real wages. For intermediate values of v, however, the reverse is true. Here, as B's citizens choose u over v, the fall in derived demand for their labour, and so in w_B/w_A, outweighs the benefit they derive from consuming u.

One way of looking at this outcome is to ask: what is the efficient use of resources in the global economy? It is inefficient, from a global perspective, to transform C's raw material into the low-quality good v, even if this can be done at zero cost (i.e. if $w_B \rightarrow 0$), as opposed to transforming it into a high-quality product, at a cost that reflects A's equilibrium wage rate. The result is that the derived demand for labour in B, which can only be used by B-firms in producing a product of low quality, falls to a degree that leads B's citizens to be worse off. Their choices as consumers create a negative effect on their prospects as suppliers of labour.

It is worth noting some factors on which this result does not depend: it holds irrespective of the number of firms in each market, and in particular it holds when this number n is large, so that we are at the 'perfect competition' limit. Thus the result is not driven by 'fixed costs' (all fixed costs are sunk in the model) or on 'imperfect competition' in product markets.

What drives the result, rather, is the combination of the two key features of the model. The first is that the preference structure of consumers is of the type described in Chapter 1, in which consumers will not purchase products offering an inferior quality-price ratio. The second is that the use of an internationally-traded raw material limits the degree to which the price of low-quality products can fall.

This 'impact' phase is, however, only the first step in the globalization process; in the next chapter, we turn to the consequences of the outcome of this phase for the incentives that drive the second ('catch-up') phase of the globalization process.

Box 3.2. What Do Managers Do?

The transfer of capabilities involves a complicated set of putative influences, whose significance, or relative importance, is hard to unravel. One of these putative influences relates to the absorbtion by the firm of 'standard managment practices'.

We've already seen how, in the auto-component sector, the achievement of high-quality levels depends crucially on the adoption of good 'working practices'. Closely linked to this, is the adoption of good procedures in production control and other areas that fall under the general heading of 'managment practices'.

In a recent pioneering study, Nick Bloom and John Van Reenen Bloom and Van Reenen (2007) have measured the degree to which a very large set of firms, across several countries, adhere to simple and widely accepted norms of 'good managment practices'. These norms comprise a wide range of items, ranging across production and quality control, financial management, human relations, and the design of incentive structures.

What the authors find is that there is a significant correlation between a firm's profitability, relative to its rivals in its industry, and the degree to which it adopts such practices.

Now correlation is not causation; it might in principle be the case that high-performing firms are more likely to hire expensive consultants who advise them to adopt such techniques. The only decisive way to address this is to set up an experiment, in which some firms in a group are randomly assigned to receive free consultancy services designed to build up standard managment practices in the firm. This is what the authors, and their collaborators, have been doing in some very recent work (as yet unpublished).

4

Globalization II: The Great Arbitrage

4.1. THE GREAT ARBITRAGE

The outcome of the process we looked at in the preceding chapter involves a liberalized trading environment, in which high capabilities in some parts of the world coexist with low wages in other areas. This provides a massive arbitrage opportunity for firms that can bring together high capabilities with low wages – and it is the exploitation of this opportunity that has been the main driver of change in the global economy over the past twenty years.

In the first half of this chapter, we look at the consequences of this process, while in the second half of the chapter we look at the underlying mechanisms that generate the transfer of capabilities across firms and countries.

The central result developed in this chapter relates to the change in the terms of trade suffered by Country A as it faces rising prices for raw materials when Country B's capabilities rise. When μ is small, so that the cost of raw materials is (much) smaller than the cost of labour, then the rise of Country B is unambiguously beneficial to Country A. Here, the citizens of Country A enjoy high-quality goods at lower prices (relative to their wage rates) and so their welfare increases. This is a phenomenon that was very evident in Europe and the United States during the 1990s, as low-price goods of increasingly high quality were imported from China.

If μ is large, however, this process of welfare improvement can go into reverse. As B's quality rises relative to A's, the rise in the derived demand for C's raw materials leads to a deterioration in the terms of trade for Country A. The rise in the raw materials cost to Country A means that the unit cost of its products rises to a point where our welfare indicator U_A falls as B's capabilities rise.

The beneficiary of this process is Country C, which is unambiguously better off. It is this process that is now attracting increasing attention in the global economy. As China becomes increasingly active in bidding up the prices of Africa's raw materials, the gain to several of the major countries of Sub-Saharan Africa is hugely significant.

In the second half of the chapter, we turn to the question of how the rise in Country B's capability is achieved. Here, the story is a complex one, since there are several mechanisms in play, and their strength and effectiveness varies hugely from one industry to another. We look, in Section 4.3, at one industry in particular in which the pace of change has been extremely fast – the car industry. By asking why this process has advanced so quickly in this industry, we can find some clues as to what factors determine the speed of effectiveness of capability transfer.

4.2. THE CONSEQUENCES OF CAPABILITY TRANSFER

We begin from the model introduced in Chapter 3, and we focus on the limiting case of interest in which $r = 0$, i.e. all goods are quality goods. We simplify by setting $c_A = c_B = 1$, in order to focus on the role of quality differences.

Setting $r = 0$, we have, following the same arguments as before, that labour demand in A and B is given by:

$$L_A^D = Mnc_A x_u = Mnx_u \quad \text{and} \quad L_B^D = Mnc_B x_v = Mnx_v$$

Again, following the same arguments as before, we have that

$$\frac{L_A^S}{L_B^S} = \frac{w_A}{w_B} = \frac{L_A^D}{L_B^D} = \frac{Mnx_u}{Mnx_v} = \frac{x_u}{x_v}$$

From (3.13), (3.14), setting $c_A = c_B = 1$, we have[1]

---

[1] This corrects an error in equation (39) of the Appendix of Sutton (2007b).

$$\frac{w_A}{w_B} = \frac{x_u}{x_v} = \frac{v}{u} \cdot \left[1 - \frac{2n-1}{n} \frac{w_A + w_C\mu}{u\left(\frac{w_A+w_C\mu}{u} + \frac{w_B+w_C\mu}{v}\right)} \right]$$

$$\div \left[1 - \frac{2n-1}{n} \frac{w_B + w_C\mu}{v\left(\frac{w_A+w_C\mu}{u} + \frac{w_B+w_C\mu}{v}\right)} \right] \quad (4.1)$$

Our focus of interest lies in asking how the wage ratio w_B/w_A and the utility indicator U_A vary as v varies between $v = u$ and its critical (threshold) value v^c.

Following the same arguments as before, we have in this zone, where A and B both produce 'quality' goods, and there are no commodity goods, i.e. $r = 0$, that[2]

$$w_C = \mu \left(\frac{w_A}{c_A} + \frac{w_B}{c_B} \right) = \mu(w_A + w_B). \quad (4.2)$$

It follows from this that the expressions involving w_C in equation (4.1) become:

$$w_A + w_C\mu = (1 + \mu^2)w_A + \mu^2 w_B$$

and

$$w_B + w_C\mu = \mu^2 w_A + (1 + \mu^2)w_B$$

This allows us to rewrite equation (4.1) as

$$\frac{w_A}{w_B} = \frac{x_u}{x_v} = \frac{v}{u} \cdot \left[1 - \frac{2n-1}{n} \frac{(1+\mu^2)w_A+\mu^2 w_B}{(1+\mu^2)w_A+\mu^2 w_B+\frac{u}{v}[\mu^2 w_A+(1+\mu^2)w_B]} \right]$$

$$\div \left[1 - \frac{2n-1}{n} \frac{\mu^2 w_A+(1+\mu^2)w_B}{\frac{v}{u}[(1+\mu^2)w_A+\mu^2 w_B]+[\mu^2 w_A+(1+\mu^2)w_B]} \right]$$

---

[2] Recall that as A uses c_A units of labour and μ units of materials to produce one unit of output, and B uses c_B units of labour and μ units of materials to produce one unit of output, and each unit of materials requires 1 unit of labour in C, we have

$$L_C^D = \mu \left(\frac{1}{c_A}L_A^D + \frac{1}{c_B}L_B^D \right)$$

and since our labour supply function implies that

$$L_A^D : L_B^D : L_C^D = L_A^S : L_B^S : L_C^S = w_A : w_B : w_C$$

equation (4.2) follows.

Writing $\frac{w_B}{w_A}$ as ω, and rearranging the expression on the r.h.s. we obtain

$$\frac{1}{\omega} = \frac{[\mu^2 + (1 + \mu^2)\omega] - \frac{n-1}{n}[(1 + \mu^2) + \mu^2\omega]\frac{v}{u}}{[(1 + \mu^2) + \mu^2\omega] - \frac{n-1}{n}[\mu^2 + (1 + \mu^2)\omega]\frac{u}{v}}$$

which reduces to the quadratic,

$$\left[(1 + \mu^2) - \frac{n-1}{n}\mu^2\frac{v}{u}\right]\omega^2 + \left[\frac{n-1}{n}(1 + \mu^2)\right]\left(\frac{u}{v} - \frac{v}{u}\right)\omega$$

$$- \left[(1 + \mu^2) - \frac{n-1}{n}\mu^2\frac{u}{v}\right] = 0 \qquad (4.3)$$

The coefficients on ω^2 and ω are both positive and decreasing in v for $v \leq u$. The third coefficient is negative for all v in the relevant range, i.e.

$$u \geq v > v^c = \frac{n-1}{n}\frac{1}{1 + 1/\mu^2}u$$

It increases in absolute value as v rises, and converges to zero as $v \to v^c$. Thus the quadratic equation (4.3) has a single positive root, ω^*, which increases with v, and as $v \to v^c$, we have $\omega^* \to 0$.[3][4]

I next examine the welfare indicator U_A as a function of v in zone 2. The welfare indicator (3.4) is

$$U_A = \frac{1}{2}\left(\frac{w_A}{M}\right)^2 \prod_{i=1}^{M}\left(\frac{u_i}{p_i}\right)^{2/M} \qquad (4.4)$$

Recall that $r = 0$ and $c_A = c_B = 1$. From the basic price equation (1.4) we have

$$\frac{p_u}{u} = \frac{p_v}{v} = \frac{n}{2n - 1}\left[\frac{w_A + w_C\mu}{u} + \frac{w_B + w_C\mu}{v}\right]$$

Writing $w_C = \mu(w_A + w_B)$ and $w_B/w_A = \omega$ as before we have

$$\frac{p_u}{u} = \frac{p_v}{v} = \frac{n}{2n - 1} \cdot w_A\{[(1 + \mu^2) + \mu^2\omega]\frac{1}{u} + [\mu^2 + (1 + \mu^2)\omega]\frac{1}{v}\}$$

$$(4.4')$$

Substituting this into the utility function (4.4) we have

[3] The argument here is analogous to that illustrated in Figure 3.3 of the preceding chapter.

[4] The 'cost differences' case can be examined in the same way, by fixing the values of u and v, and examining the behaviour of w_B/w_A as c_B rises, holding c_A constant. Here, the wage ratio remains positive for all c_B, falling asymptotically to zero as $c_B \to \infty$.

$$U_A(v; u) = \frac{1}{2M^2} \left(\frac{2n-1}{n} \right)^2 \frac{1}{\{[(1+\mu^2) + \mu^2 \omega]\frac{1}{u} + [\mu^2 + (1+\mu^2)\omega]\frac{1}{v}\}^2}$$

$$(4.5)$$

Combining the solution for ω from (4.3) with (4.5), the behaviour of U_A as a function v over the range $v^C \le v \le u$ can be checked.

Two special cases are of particular interest:

(a) when v lies below its critical value v^C, Country B is inactive and $\omega = 0$. Setting $v = v^C = \frac{n-1}{n} \frac{1}{1+1/\mu^2} u$ and $\omega = 0$ in (4.5), and simplifying, we obtain

$$U_A(0; u) = \frac{1}{2M^2} \left(\frac{n-1}{n} \right)^2 \frac{1}{\{(1+\mu^2)\frac{1}{u}\}^2} \tag{4.6}$$

(b) when $v = u$, we have $\omega = 1$, and (4.5) becomes

$$U_A(u; u) = \frac{1}{2M^2} \left(\frac{2n-1}{n} \right)^2 \frac{1}{\{2(1+2\mu^2)\frac{1}{u}\}^2} \tag{4.7}$$

The question of interest is: is the welfare indicator U_A raised or lowered by B's presence?

Comparing (4.6) and (4.7), we see that $U_A(u; u) \gtreqless U_A(0; u)$ according as

$$\frac{2n-1}{2(1+2\mu^2)} \gtreqless \frac{n-1}{1+\mu^2}$$

which is equivalent to

$$\mu \lesseqgtr \frac{1}{\sqrt{2n-3}} \tag{4.8}$$

This relation is shown in Figure 4.1. (Recall that a maintained assumption is that the number of firms in each industry in each country, n, is at least 2.) To the right of the schedule shown, the presence of an equally capable competitor B lowers the value of the welfare indicator U_A.

The full schedule $U_A(v; u)$ is shown in Figure 4.2. It is not, in all cases, monotonic.

The intuition is as follows: recall that our welfare indicator measures the welfare of 'workers', and excludes profit income. B's presence has two effects:

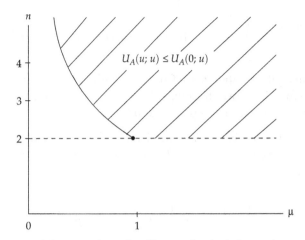

Fig. 4.1. Capability Transfer and Welfare. In the shaded area, the presence of an equally capable competitor B lowers the value of the welfare indicator U_A. Recall that n is assumed to be greater or equal to 2 throughout.

(i) It causes prices to fall relative to wage rates. This effect is similar to the welfare-raising effect of trade in the standard 'monopolistic competition' models of Krugman (1979) and others, as described in Chapter 1, and in Chapter 2 (recall in particular Figure 3.4, with $v = u$).

(ii) As B's quality rises, it exerts increasing demand for raw materials from C. This causes A's terms of trade to deteriorate, in the sense that A pays a higher price for raw material inputs, relative to the price of its output.

We can now interpret the pattern of results shown in Figures 4.1 and 4.2. When μ is close to zero, effect (i) dominates, and B's presence raises U_A. When μ is high, effect (ii) dominates, and B's presence lowers U_A. For intermediate cases, the effect can go in either direction. For example, in the case where $n = 2$ and $\mu = 1$, as shown in Figure 4.2, a rise in v above v^c initially lowers U_A, but this effect is offset as v rises towards u; in this example, we have $U_A(u; u) = U_A(0; u)$ as is easily checked by substituting $n = 2$ and $\mu = 1$ in (4.8).

Once μ is sufficiently large, then, the rise in the derived demand for raw materials from Country C will lead to a fall in the welfare of advanced countries as B catches up on A.

In early discussions of China's impact on global markets, the 'cheap final goods' effect (i) was much more remarked upon. Only recently, as

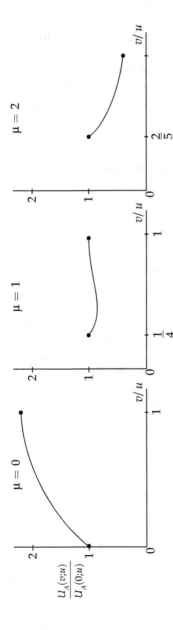

Fig. 4.2. The Welfare Impact of Capability Transfer

Notes: The figure shows the welfare indicator $U_A(v; u)$ expressed as a ratio to welfare in the absence of Country B, denoted $U_A(0; u)$, as a function of B's relative quality v/u, over the range $\frac{v}{u}|_{crit} \leq \frac{v}{u} \leq 1$. If v/u lies at or below $\frac{v}{u}|_{crit}$, U_A coincides with $U_A(0; u)$. The curves are drawn for $n = 2$.

its expansion leads it to play an increasingly important role in global markets for raw materials, has the 'raw materials prices' effect (ii) attracted more attention.

While the model is designed to pull apart the two effects in the simplest setting, it should be stressed that in reality most countries are *both* suppliers of raw materials and exporters of final goods. So which effect dominates in practice? A helpful insight can be obtained by looking at the change in the terms of trade for advanced industrial economies over the past 20 years. For the US there has been no marked change; the same is true of Germany, France, and the UK. But Japan, which relies very heavily on imported raw materials, has seen a secular decline in its terms of trade (Figure 4.3).

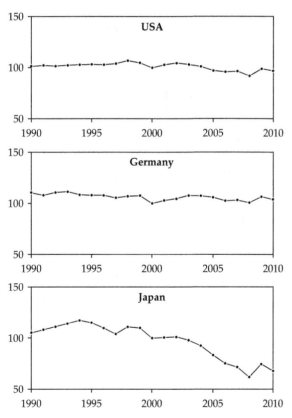

Fig. 4.3. Terms of Trade for the USA, Germany, and Japan (base year: 2000)

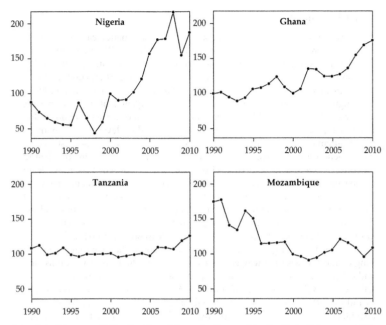

Fig. 4.4. Terms of Trade for Selected Countries in Sub-Saharan Africa (base year: 2000)

But what of the raw materials producers themselves? It is easy to show, following the same form of argument as we used above, that the welfare indicator of Country C rises as B's quality rises from $v = v^c$ to $v = u$ (Appendix 4.1).

The consequences of this for the raw materials producers of Sub-Saharan Africa, have already been remarked upon in Section 4.1 above. The changing terms of trade for a number of Sub-Saharan countries is shown in Figure 4.4. Those countries that are heavy exporters of oil or minerals have seen an improvement in their terms of trade. This is true of Nigeria and Ghana, for example – but it is not true for those countries that have little or no exports of oil and minerals.

Box 4.1. Why Benchmark Quality?

One of the most heated economic controversies of the 1990s related to the notion of 'competitiveness'. At the heart of the debate was the question: does it make economic sense to assess the 'competitiveness' of a country against other countries?

Box 4.1. (**continued**)

But what does 'competitiveness' mean? As the debate made clear, the word was used by different commentators to mean different things. The most influential contribution was that of Paul Krugman, whose position became widely familiar to economists and non-economists alike when his several articles on the subject were reprinted in his best-selling book, *Pop Internationalism* Krugman (1997).

Krugman sets out his view by reference to a sequence of models, that are closely similar to the 'world of widgets' of Chapter 1 above. There are no quality differences, and firms and countries differ only in their levels of productivity. As Krugman explains, a firm's viability in competing against its domestic rivals will depend on its relative productivity, and it will make sense for the *firm* to be concerned about its *relative* level of productivity. But when we move from comparing firms to comparing countries, this is no longer so. For countries' wage levels will adjust to reflect their productivity levels, and a country's unit wage cost (which we can think of in this context as its 'competitiveness') depends both on its productivity and its wage level. What matters to the country's welfare is its *absolute* level of productivity, not its level relative to other countries.

Now this line of argument continues to hold good when we move from the 'single industry' world of widgets, to a setting where there are many industries, and different countries have different patterns of productivity. Some countries will be relatively productive in industry A while others are relatively better in industry B. At equilibrium, each will specialize in its area of comparative advantage – and, as Krugman explains, it will still be the case that a country's level of welfare will depend primarily (subject only to some secondary qualifications) on its own absolute level of productivity in those industries in which it is active.

In this world, as Krugman emphasizes, a concern about 'competitiveness' is an unwelcome distraction from what a government should be concerned to foster: the absolute levels of productivity across firms and industries.

Now the above discussion does *not* mean that a country's welfare is unaffected by productivity improvements occurring in other countries; Krugman explains this point by reference to long-established propositions in standard international trade theory. (We can see this in the present model in Figure 4.2.)

So what is there to add? I will deliberately avoid the troublesome ambiguity of the word 'competitiveness', and I will confine my attention to the distinct and narrower question: does quality benchmarking, i.e. the measurement of *relative* quality, make sense at the level of an industry or an economy (as opposed to the – uncontroversial – level of an individual firm)?

My aim in this chapter has been to explain what is new when we turn to a world in which (a) goods differ in quality, and 'bad products cannot drive out good' (Chapter 1) and (b) the production of these goods requires inputs that are themselves internationally tradeable (Chapter 3). In this setting, there is something new, relative to the world of widgets. As we have seen in equation (3.31), it is now the case, even at the level of a country rather than at the level of a firm, that *relative* quality matters. The viability of all 'quality' industries in country B depends on the *ratio* of its quality to that of country A: it is the *ratio* v/u that must exceed some critical level in order for country B's products to be viable.

So in this world, it makes sense for country *B* to benchmark its quality levels vis-à-vis international rivals, and to be concerned at a national level about the *relative* quality of its manufacturing industries.

To take an extreme case for the sake of illustration: suppose, as in the text, that almost all goods are 'quality' goods. Then if *A*'s level of quality *u* is higher, it follows that country *B* will need to have a correspondingly high value of *v* to meet the threshold ratio (3.31). Below this level of relative quality, its GDP per capita will remain at an arbitrarily low level.

So what is going on here? What has changed, relative to the world of widgets? The best way to see what is new here, is to note that the manufacturing firm in the world of widgets is transforming local labour into final goods. All that matters to its GDP per capita is the number of widgets obtained per hour of labour utilized. But in the world we are looking at in this chapter, we can think of a manufacturing firm as transforming a unit of homogeneous raw material into a unit of final product of a certain quality. It is efficient, in terms of the global economy, that this transformation is carried out by firms and countries that can carry it out at a high level of quality. Once globally traded inputs are needed, price cannot fall below a threshold of unit materials cost that is independent of the local wage rate. But this means that the quality offered has to be high enough to support a price that covers this lowest possible price level: and this minimum acceptable threshold is a *relative* quality level.

So once we are in a world characterized by features (a) and (b) above, it is quite appropriate that attention be focussed at a national level on benchmarking *relative* quality not only at the level of the firm, but at the level of the industry, or the economy.

4.3. THE TRANSFER OF CAPABILITIES

In this section, we turn to the question of *how* the capabilities of *B* rise towards those of *A*, and in particular to the role played by the transfer of capabilities across firms and countries.

The transfer of capabilities involves two intertwined elements. One relates to purely technological know-how or engineering expertise. The second relates to 'working practices'. The latter element is always crucial to the attainment of high-quality levels, whereas the former becomes relatively more important as we move from the less technically demanding industries (such as clothing) to more technically demanding industries (such as semiconductors).

The economics literature has traditionally emphasized the role of 'technological know-how'. The management literature, however, has been heavily concerned with understanding the role played by 'good working practices'. The most influential example of the importance of good working practices comes from the car industry, where the Toyota company developed new and better methods of working in the 1970s. One example of Toyota's rich menu of inter-related practices related to quality control. Instead of having a quality control person checking items at the end of a production line, the idea was to have all members of a team understand each other's tasks, and to check the quality of their individual input before passing it on to a co-worker. This avoids the problem of devoting additional work to an item that is already defective. Toyota's rich menu of practices, of which this is just a single isolated example, deeply influenced other car makers, first in Japan, and then in the US and Europe, during the 1980s. By the 1990s, these practices had become uniform across the international car industry, to an extraordinary degree.[5]

4.4. THE SPEED AND EFFECTIVENESS OF TRANSFER I: VERTICAL RELATIONSHIPS

The car industry provides a useful point of departure in exploring the speed and effectiveness of transfer. The industry comprises a relatively small number of car makers (assemblers), and a vast network of component suppliers. In this industry, the transfer of capabilities has been astonishingly fast and effective. In China's and India's car industries, those component suppliers who sell directly to the car makers ('first-tier suppliers'), both domestic and foreign-owned, had within 7–8 years of the arrival of the main wave of international car makers attained 'world-class' standards of quality and productivity by 2003, as measured by conventional defect rates in parts supplied (Sutton, 2004: Figure 4.5).

The reason for the effectiveness of this capability transfer appears to involve two factors:

(i) As we have just seen, the auto sector is unusual in the degree to which a common set of business practices and production routines have become standardized. This has produced an institutional structure in the international industry in which transfers are facilitated.

---

[5] The classic book on this subject is *The Machine that Changed the World* (Womack, Jones, and Roos, 1990). See also Clark and Fujimoto (1991).

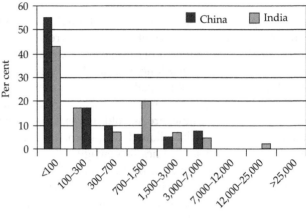

Fig. 4.5. Supplier Defect Rates for a Twinned Pair of New-Generation Carmakers in China and India

Notes: The defect rates relate to parts supplied to the car maker ('extended defect rates'). The rate is measured as a number of defective components per million components supplied.

Practices have become so codified that independent specialist consulting firms have emerged, to whom car makers can refer potential suppliers, in order to help them 'get into the window'; and

(ii) Transfers of capability within a 'vertical' (i.e. supply chain) setting tend to be relatively effective in general. This presumably reflects the close alignment of incentives: the auto-maker sees it as profitable in the long run to have a number of high-quality, low-cost suppliers for each (set of) component(s), while the supplier stands to gain from its enhanced capability in the context of future contracts with various car makers. In practice, the auto-maker advises and incentivizes its many suppliers, in a process that involves the back-and-forth movement of engineers and managers between the two firms.

In contrast to the case of India's car industry, the process of adjustment in the Indian machine tool industry, which we looked at earlier, and where conditions (i) and (ii) above are not present, has been extremely slow and difficult (Sutton, 2001).

But a focus on the role of vertical relations and incentives, while it captures the case of the auto industry quite nicely, falls far short of an adequate account of the determinants of the speed and effectiveness of capability transfer. To see this, consider the way things work in the clothing (apparel) sector, where the industry again has a 'vertical' structure, but where the number of final sellers (retailers) is quite enormous, relative to the number of car makers. Here, a highly developed institutional structure has long been in place that joins up low-cost manufacturers with leading retailers in high-income countries.

The clothing industry is driven by the vagaries of ever-changing fashion; and the key capabilities are twofold. The first lies in operating a manufacturing business that allows for rapid changes in the clothing lines produced. The second lies in managing the supply chains between manufacturer and retailer. The institutional framework of the industry involves two channels: international trade fairs – such as the annual Singapore fair – allow many players on both sides of the market to meet. In parallel to this channel, leading retailers take the initiative in seeking out potential manufacturers directly.[6]

Now in supply chains of this type, a manufacturer can easily be linked into the international supply chain once it meets some standards of quality and reliability – and these latter capabilities are not very difficult to develop. The most striking instance of capability transfer in this context comes from Bangladesh, where scores of producers of basic cotton T-shirts entered the market in the 1990s, to the point where Bangladesh became the world's largest supplier of cotton T-shirts (Mostafa and Klepper, 2011).

But the role of supply chains in transferring capability in this sector goes beyond the development of manufacturing processes. More importantly, it lies in the transfer of know-how and information from retailers to manufacturers. The Ever-Glory company in South-east China is a young firm that grew very rapidly in the 1990s: its key turning point lay in obtaining a contract to supply a Japanese department store. These stores are known in the industry as the industry's most demanding clients. By learning to meet the quality demands of its Japanese customer, the Ever-Glory company achieved quality levels in manufacturing and delivery that set it apart from its many local rivals (Brandt, Rawski, and Sutton, 2008, Chapter 15).

---

[6] Unsurprisingly, there is an opportunity here for a middleman, who writes contracts with many manufacturers for their capacity over a certain period, and who then contracts with retailers to supply that capacity to meet their ever-fluctuating needs: the Li&Fung company of Hong Kong has built a leading position in this respect.

This process of learning within vertical relations extends to the long-understood[7] role played by equipment suppliers: the Shagang steel firm in China achieved major advances in capability over the past twenty years by way of a close interaction with its German equipment suppliers Fuchs (Brandt, Rawski, and Sutton, 2008, p. 598). As the firm installed new equipment, its suppliers' engineers interacted with its in-home team to push the technology further, to the benefit of both companies.

So one factor that appears to play a systematic role in fostering rapid transfer, in several different ways, is the presence of vertical buyer–seller relations in the industry. Indeed, in econometric studies of the impact of FDI on an industry's performance, one theme that emerges is that *vertical* transfer of this kind has a substantial impact.[8]

4.5. THE SPEED AND EFFECTIVENESS OF TRANSFER II: ABSORBTIVE CAPACITY AND WORKING PRACTICES

The second factor that merits attention in this context relates to the 'Absorptive Capacity' of Country B's industry – and the pursuit of this issue will bring us to the heart of the 'capability' concept.

The idea of 'absorptive capacity' Cohen and Levinthal (1990) posits that the cost of reaching capability level u is lower, according as v is higher. This seems a plausible assumption, though it will not necessarily hold in all circumstances (Box 4.1).

Box 4.2. FDI Destinations

Suppose, for the moment, that the 'Absorbtive Capacity' hypothesis of Cohen and Levinthal (1990) is correct. Then, the question arises: if there are several 'B-type' countries with different levels of v, which of these offers the best returns to transfers? A lower level of v is associated with a lower relative wage rate, so there are two countervailing considerations. The most favoured location might in principle lie, in terms of Figure 3.4, anywhere on the interior of the segment running from $v = u$ down to the critical level of v below which B's relative

---

[7] Von Hippel (1994).

[8] Javorcik (2004). On the other hand, there is a long-standing hypothesis that suggests the foreign firm might have a positive effect on its local rivals within the same industry ('horizontal spillovers'): this, however, receives little support from the data.

Box 4.2. (**continued**)

wage reaches its minimum value. It is worth noting that countries with v below this critical value are strictly dominated as destinations. The poorer countries unambiguously benefit from the impact effect of liberalization, since they have very small levels of employment in the 'quality goods' industries, and so the scope for losses on this account is limited. (The losses suffered by the middle-income countries in Figure 3.4 come from a fall in the derived demand for labour from their 'quality goods' industries.) But if the Absorbtive Capacity hypothesis is valid, these countries may not advance further during the transfer process. This observation has great relevance to the experience of many Sub-Saharan African countries in the 1990s, a point to which we will return in Chapter 5.

Absorbtive Capacity is of great importance in a sophisticated manufacturing operation such as the building of car engines. An engine maker is likely to value highly the availability of a highly qualified engineering workforce, either within a firm that can become a joint-venture partner, or within a local labour market where experienced workers can be hired. This is nicely illustrated by the experience of the Germany's Audi company, when it decided to outsource engine production to a lower cost environment. Having considered some eighty potential locations, the company settled on Gyor, in Hungary. One of the key factors favouring Gyor, was the availability of a highly qualified engineering workforce. In a more technically demanding operation, where high levels of technical expertise are needed, then bringing an existing technically qualified workforce up to speed is preferable to the seat-makers preferred strategy of hiring inexperienced workers and building up expertise from scratch.

In contrast to the engine makers, the manufacturers of less technically demanding auto components such as car seats or exhausts may take a very different view (Sutton 2004). Conventional wisdom among seat makers is that starting with a new workforce on a greenfield site is a major advantage: one executive based at the world headquarters of a multinational car seat maker remarked that he would expect to be able to achieve world-class quality standards at a greenfield plant in any country within one year of its establishment. If, however, he was operating in a joint venture with an established local seat maker, the process might take three years. Sutton (2004) found for example that:

- A multinational seat maker operating on a greenfield site in India had an initial external defect rate of 2,085 parts per million (the 'world-class' threshold is 100 parts per million). By the firm's third year of operation, the rate had fallen to sixty-five parts per million, close to the fifty parts per million level regarded as 'award class' by multinational seat makers.

- One of the leading domestic seat makers in India began to introduce international best-practice procedures in the mid-1990s. Beginning from an initial external defect rate of 20, 000 parts per million, it took five years of steadily improving performance to bring the figure down to its 2003 level of 200 parts per million.

The difference between these two cases reflects the slowness of 'relearning': if established routines are in place, it is hard to change them; beginning from scratch is easier.

Among multinational seat and exhaust makers, engineers from high-performing plants are regularly transferred to newly formed joint ventures with established domestic producers. One engineer, who had been seconded from a world-class greenfield plant in India to a recently established joint-venture plant in China, remarked that his six-month stint would be 'largely a matter of talking'. It was not the obvious alterations to the physical plant that mattered, he remarked, but rather inducing a shift in work practices. At the most elementary level, this involves a move away from traditional notions of 'inspection at the end of the production line' to a system in which each operator along the line searches for defects in each seat section as it arrives and as it departs. The idea of such constant monitoring is to avoid 'adding value to defective units' and to set the basis for a system in which the sources of defects are quickly identified and rectified.

What is at issue, then, is the question of 'working practices'. A firm's capability is not built on 'know-how' alone: it also depends on the presence of good working practices. Indeed, as we move from the more technically demanding operation ('engine manufacture') to less technically demanding operation ('car seats'), the *relative* importance of working practices in determining productivity and quality becomes greater.

And here we come to the key point about the building and transfer of capability: were capability simply a matter of 'know-how', it could be transferred quickly and efficiently via blueprints and manuals. It is precisely because much of what matters involves tacit knowledge (Von Hippel, 1994), or working practices, that are difficult to transfer, that the process is slow and difficult.

The manpower involved in these transfers can be minimal, but the timescale involved may vary from several months to several years.

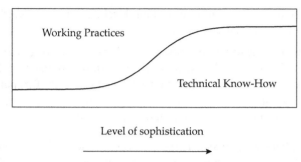

Fig. 4.6. Elements of Capability

In the case of the Bangladeshi T-shirt makers, Mostafa and Klepper (2011) found that a substantial advance in productivity and quality was associated with the hiring of a single engineer from a 'high capability' firm in the industry.

In some firms, it may be so difficult to alter old working habits acquired over many years that a radical alternative may prove to be more effective, as the following example shows.

In the mid-1990s, a newly retired CEO of one of India's leading companies took over a failing engineering firm, with the brief to 'close it down within eighteen months'. Staffed by predominantly middle-aged men, heavily unionized, and with a product line that was becoming obsolete, the firm appeared to have little future. The CEO, however, decided on a radical solution. He began by hiring twenty seventeen year olds who had never worked in the industry, half male and half female. He taught the group to make a standard 'steering knuckle', a job that requires considerable care both in machining and assembly. He then found an American joint-venture partner, with whom he obtained an order for 2.5 million units from one of the leading US car makers. The venture was a huge success (Sutton 2004). Armed with this example of the effectiveness of following good working practices, he returned to the main factory with some suggestions ...

It is this challenging task of changing working practices that is the most pressing challenge in the low- and mid-level manufacturing industries in the developing countries. The challenge associated with 'technological know-how' assumes a dominant role only as we move towards the more sophisticated end of the manufacturing spectrum (Sutton and Kellow, 2010).

4.6. PIGGYBACKING THE SUPPLY CHAIN

One of the most crucial indirect benefits of the recent wave of international joint ventures in the car industry lies in the fact that these ventures stimulate the development of capabilities in the domestic supply chain, allowing domestic car makers to benefit from new possibilities in outsourcing from low-price, high-quality suppliers. Perhaps the most striking instance of the mechanism in an Indian context is the case of Mahindra and Mahindra, one of India's leading producers of commercial vehicles and tractors. In 1994 the company went through a major restructuring, one outcome of which was a new policy shift in favour of substantial outsourcing of components and sub-assemblies. Over the following four years, virtually all components other than engines, transmission systems, and body (skin) panels began to be outsourced. For engines' the head and block were bought in from a local supplier in semifinished form; all transmission components were bought in. For rear axles the centre bracket was bought in as a casting and machined in-house, but the tubes and shafts were bought from local suppliers in fully finished form.

This shift towards reliance on the local supply chain came to a peak with the firm's introduction of the Scorpio van, a light multi-use vehicle launched in 1998. The Scorpio van was designed in-house, using an Italian design house as a consultant on styling. The outsourcing policy was pushed to new levels, with a network of 110 local suppliers. This network allowed the company to reduce unit production costs by much more than they otherwise could have, and it allowed the Scorpio to be sold at an ex-dealer price (including air conditioning and power steering) of 5.5 lakh rupees ($11,000), about 60 per cent of the price expected by industry observers at the time of its launch. Sales of the Scorpio have transformed the financial fortunes of Mahindra and Mahindra during the five years since its launch.

4.7. GOING IT ALONE

So far, we've looked at the catch-up process (in terms of the theory, the rise of B's quality level v) as being driven by a transfer of technical know-how and working practices from Country A to Country B. But the liberalization of the global market, even in the absence of such transfer, leads to enhanced incentives for in-house innovation by firms in Country *B* – for these firms now face a situation in which the profit to be gained from any given rise in their quality is greater, as they now sell into the larger, global market.

The way in which the changing competition environment, and the new access to global markets, may affect investments in capability building is well illustrated by the cases of two Indian firms that leapt to the forefront of their respective industries.

Bharat Forge was a long-established forgings company, working in a 'commodity' type industry and making poor returns. Beginning in the late 1990s, it established itself as one of the global top five firms in specialist forgings. It did this by inventing, in-house, a new suite of computer software that allowed the firm to estimate numerically, on the basis of a blueprint of a forged part, the number of blows it would take to finish the item. This obviated the need to create the extremely costly die for the part, in order to find out how many blows were involved, and so what the unit cost of production of the forged part would be. This put the company at a crucial advantage in getting its bids for specialist forging jobs right, and marked the start of its ascent to the global top five.

A second example arises in the machine tool industry, which was suffering from intense import competition during the 1990s. In this case, it was not access to the large global market that drove the change, but rather the increasing intensity of competition that globalization brought to India's domestic market. Set up by four disaffected local engineers, ACE Designers focussed on designing and producing a single, top-selling product: a basic (two-axis, single spindle) computer-controlled lathe.[9] It took some years to reach quality levels that were very close to those of the main competing imports (from Taiwan), i.e. to 'get into the window'. Once that was achieved, the company began a series of price cuts, arguing that, while Indian buyers would be insensitive to price cuts if the quality gap was large, this would cease to be the case once the quality gap was small. This proved to be the case: price cuts led to large rises in sales volume, thus reducing unit production costs, and opening the way for more price cuts. ACE

---

[9] i.e. there was a single chuck to hold and rotate the metal being machined, and it moved horizontally and vertically.

Designers had, by 2001, won a 70 per cent share of the Indian market for computer-controlled lathes.

4.8. SUMMING UP

Phase II of globalization involves the marrying up of high capabilities in one part of the world with low wages in other parts of the world. We saw above how this process affects welfare in the advanced industrial economies ('*A*'), in the industrializing countries ('*B*'), and in the raw materials rich countries ('*C*'). We have also looked at the more analytically complex question of how the growth in, and transfer of, capabilities from *A* to *B* comes about. Here, an analytical codification of the issues involved is made difficult by the fact that there are many channels involved (FDI, outsourcing, 'go-it-alone' responses), and there are many industry-specific factors that affect the speed and effectiveness of transfer (codification of knowledge, incentive effects in vertical relationships).

In the next chapter we turn to the question of how firms, in this globalized environment, face new incentives to further develop their own capabilities. The return to R&D on product development is enhanced by firms' new access to a globalized market – and the responses of firms to this incentive sparks off a new wave of escalation in capability building.[10] This is the same process that we saw in Chapter 1, Section 1.5, which led to the 'nonconvergence' result, and showed that even in the large global economy, some capabilities will necessarily remain relatively scarce. It is the intensification of this process in a globalized world that is the subject of the next chapter.

Box 4.3. Globalization and Inequality

Does globalization increase inequality? This was one of the most contentious issues in the globalization debates of the 1990s. Certainly, inequality has increased within some of the advanced industrial economies over the past two decades. In the United States, this increase has been driven by a rising income share for the top 1 per cent of the population – but this is in large part driven by

---

[10] There is a useful analytical simplification involved here, in listing the three phases of globalization 'sequentially'. In practice, Phases II and III overlap in time: many firms anticipate the changed incentives and quickly intensify their capability-building efforts.

Box 4.3. (continued)

factors such as the escalating levels of CEO compensation, that have no clear link to globalization. But there is one mechanism that seems to play a significant role in linking globalization to inequality within countries: the widening gap between the pay of unskilled workers and that of skilled workers. Krugman (1997) reviews the economics of this issue at a general level; here, we look at the most revealing empirical study of the issue, that of Verhoogen (2008).

In the model of the main text, we take all workers to be identical. Verhoogen's model has two groups of workers, skilled and unskilled. He uses a simple production function in which one unit of output requires one unit of unskilled labour and one unit of skilled labour. Skilled workers differ in their skill levels, and the quality of the product rises with this skill level.

He assumes further that firms themselves differ in their levels of capability, so that the quality of a firm's product now depends both on the firm's capability and on the skill level of its skilled workers. Firms can sell on the domestic market, or on the global (export) market. The final step is to posit that, on the global (export) market, consumers' willingness-to-pay for any given improvement in quality is greater than that on the domestic market. At equilibrium, firms will choose to be exporters, or to confine their sales to the (lower price, lower quality) domestic market. The way firms partition themselves into these two types emerges as part of the equilibrium of the model: there is a critical threshold of capability. Firms above this threshold level export; those below it do not.

Using this framework, Verhoogen examines the way in which Mexican industries responded to the (exogenous shock of) the peso devaluation of 1994. The effect of this devaluation is to make the value (in pesos) of products exported to the US (or other export markets) higher, relative to goods sold domestically. So more firms choose to export (the critical threshold of capability shifts downwards). Moreover, those firms that do export now seek to raise further their levels of quality (since the return in pesos to an increase in quality, that can be achieved by paying a higher wage, in pesos, to their skilled workers, is greater than it was before devaluation). The result, both in the model, and in Verhoogen's empirical findings, is a widening gap between the (lower) wage of unskilled workers, and that of the skilled workers.

What makes Verhoogen's paper valuable is that it provides, in microcosm, a picture of the mechanism through which the opening up of countries to the international economy can lead to rising inequality. If we accept the assumption that higher quality levels are (more easily) achieved through the employment of workers from the high wage, high ability end of the labour market, then opening up the economy to a global market in which a higher premium attaches to higher quality products, then it is indeed possible in principle that globalization can increase inequality – and the Verhoogen study indicates that this channel of influence may be of some significant size in practice.

5

Globalization III: The Moving Window

5.1. THE MOVING WINDOW REVISITED

In Chapter 1, I introduced the idea of a 'window' defined in terms of the firm's wage-adjusted capability u/wc, i.e. the reciprocal of the firm's 'effective cost level' (Figure 1.6, and Figure 5.1 below). We saw in Chapter 2 that the process of trade liberalization leads to an upward shift in the threshold level of the wage-adjusted capability required for a firm to be viable in the global market (Figure 5.1, labelled (a)). In this chapter, we'll see that the third phase of globalization leads to an upward shift in the top of the window, defined as the highest level of the wage-adjusted capability in the global market (Figure 5.1, labelled (b)). The process through which this happens is essentially the same process of 'escalation' in firms' spending in capability building that we saw in Chapter 1 (Section 1.5). Now, however, things are a bit more complex.

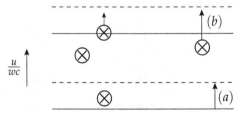

Fig. 5.1. The Moving Window Revisited. Trade Liberalization causes the bottom of the window to move up (a), while the intensification of competition in capability building among all surviving firms causes the top of the window, defined by the highest level of u/wc among the firms, to rise (b).

In the first half of this chapter, we are concerned with technological competition among firms whose efforts redefine the top of the window. In the second half of the chapter, we shift our attention to the opposite end of the spectrum. Here, our focus is on those firms and countries that were more or less left behind when global markets began to liberalize during the 1990s and who now face the challenge of 'getting into the window'. It is here that we meet with the challenges, and the new-found hopes, of the economies of Sub-Saharan Africa.

5.2. ESCALATING AGAIN

Phase III involves firms reassessing their investments in capability building. Following the catch-up process of Phase II, there are more 'high-capability' firms in each market. The market shares of the old market leaders have been squeezed, and the returns from incremental investments in R&D are now enhanced. The intuition for this is the same as that underlying the 'non-convergence theorem' of Chapter 1: if we have a large(r) number of firms with small(er) market shares, then the benefit of jumping ahead and capturing some given level of market share is greater.[1] There is, then, a new phase of investment in capability building, and this will affect all firms. Different firms will escalate to different degrees, and not all of these escalations will lead to a new 'highest' level of wage-adjusted capability u/wc. But as the process continues, at least one firm will breach the barrier, as we will see below – leading to the upward shift in the window shown in Figure 5.1.

Box 5.1. Capability Building: what is $F(u)$?

The model set out in Chapter 1 (Section 1.6) assumes a relationship between the 'demand shifter' u and the fixed and sunk cost F invested in 'capability building'. In practice, this cost F can take many forms.

The most familiar and conventional example, and the one that is most familiar from the Industrial Organization literature, treats F as the financial outlay made by the firm on Research and Development. But F can as easily stand for the cost of advertising outlays, with u now representing the strength of the firm's brand image Sutton (1991).

---

[1] For a full analysis of the way in which the intensity of price competition interacts with the incentives to invest, in this setting, see Symeonidis (2002).

But there are some less obvious, but no less important, possibilities. Consider, for instance, a maker of auto-components from one of Eastern Europe's 'transition economies' in the 1990s, who approaches a multinational car maker. Given the absence of a well-developed local auto-industry supply chain, it may be difficult to convince the car maker of the supplier's likely quality. To win its first international contract, the parts maker is likely to settle for a very poor financial deal – effectively losing money on the contract. But once the two firms strike a deal, the to-and-fro of engineers between the parts maker and the car maker will lead to a substantial transfer of capabilities (see Chapter 4), and this transfer of know-how will mean the parts maker's capability will be higher and its track record in becoming a supplier to the multinational car maker provides a reliable signal of quality, thus allowing it to achieve more profitable terms of contracts with other car makers in the future.

In this example, F has become, not a financial outlay, but an opportunity cost: for the parts maker could have made different parts for some alternative, less demanding, buyer – and in so doing, made more profit in the short term, at the expense of making no improvement in its capability.

The analysis of investing in capability in Phase III is more complex than that set out in Section 1.5 above. The initial conditions now take the form of a set of capabilities inherited from Phase II. Second, sunk costs have been invested by firms in reaching some level of capability, and the choice is between spending zero, and remaining at that level, or investing incrementally to raise u further.

The reader is referred to Sutton (2007b) for a treatment of Phase III, based on a general equilibrium version of the model of Section 1.5. Here, I summarize the results of that analysis.

A 'general' treatment of the issue would be rather unwieldy, as it would have to consider all possible configurations of capabilities that might emerge at the end of Phase II. We focus here on some special cases that throw light on the nature of the economic mechanisms involved.

It is intuitively obvious that if B's initial capability is low and the catch-up process in Phase II is weak, then B's weakness may be maintained in the third phase.[2] The question I focus on here relates to the opposite scenario: what kind of final outcome will emerge in the situation where the catch-up process of Phase II is strong? To address

---

[2] This effect is analogous to that explored by Stokey (1991) in the context of a dynamic quality competition model. A similar effect arises in the context of a learning-by-doing model in Young (1991).

this question, I focus on the 'full catch-up' setting in which country B comes to match A's levels of productivity and quality at the end of Phase II. Given the increase in the size of the global market available to firms, it will now be profitable for at least some firms to make new investments in capability building. The question we focus on is this: will this process lead to a 'shakeout' of firms, or will all $2n$ firms now present in each industry survive?

To motivate what follows, it is worth recalling the general ('non-convergence') property common to models of the present kind: if the countries were united *ab initio* into a (large) single market, so that all firms' initial investments were made in the light of this, then the number of firms entering each industry would be the same, independently of the size of the market. This suggests that we might expect some shakeout to occur among the $2n$ firms now active in each market. What makes matters more complicated here, is that the fixed outlays incurred by firms in achieving their initial quality level v (and any fixed outlays incurred in a process of transfer of capabilities) are sunk; and this tends to work against shakeout.

The question of interest, then, is: will the process of reinvestment lead to a 'shakeout' of firms? A full analysis is beyond my present scope; here, I focus on the 'best case' scenario from the point of country B, i.e. that in which catch-up is complete, so that the firms begin from a symmetric situation in which, in each industry, n firms in A and n firms in B all offer the same quality u (and both countries have the same wage rate).

In Sutton (2007b), I recast the analysis of Chapter 1, Section 1.5 in general equilibrium setting. I consider a two-stage game, in the first stage of which each firm decides on a non-negative level of incremental investment, while the second stage involves Cournot competition as before.

Recall the basic cost function of Chapter 1, Section 1.5,

$$F(u) = u^\beta, \quad u \geq 1, \ \beta \geq 1$$

where $1/\beta$ represents the elasticity of response of quality u to fixed and sunk outlays F. (Recall that a low value of β means that quality responds strongly to fixed and sunk outlays, and so to a high level of concentration, so that the market is dominated by a small number of firms.)

In Phase III, firms in either country can raise their quality to some new level $\tilde{u} \geq u$, and pay an incremental sunk cost

$$F(\tilde{u}|u) = \tilde{u}^{\beta} - u^{\beta}. \tag{5.1}$$

The outcome depends critically on the value of β. The equilibrium is not, in general, unique. An equilibrium outcome may take one of two forms: in each type of equilibrium, some sub-set of the firms reinvest, while the remaining firms make no additional investment. The first form of outcome involves the remaining firms becoming inactive ('shakeout'). Here, the high investors have jumped to such a high level of u that the non-investors are no longer 'in the window'. In the second form of outcome, the non-investing firms continue to earn positive sales revenue in equilibrium ('no shakeout').

It is when β is low (i.e. the industry has few firms), that the outcome takes the first form ('shakeout'). When β is high, the jump in quality by reinvesting firms is relatively small, and the remaining firms remain active ('no shakeout'). In the model of Sutton (2007b), for example:

- For $1 < \beta \leq 2$ (whence $n = 2$), there exists a symmetric equilibrium in which exactly one firm survives in A and one in B, while the remaining firms make no additional investment and are inactive at equilibrium.

- For $\beta > 5$, there is no (symmetric) equilibrium outcome that involves shakeout.

What this suggests, then, is that in all but the most globally concentrated industries, the legacy of the pre-globalization phase is to leave in place more firms than would otherwise be in operation; but that in these most highly concentrated markets, a process of shakeout will eliminate this effect.

The welfare gain enjoyed by countries in Phase III derives from the rise in equilibrium quality, and it is when β is low (i.e. the global market is highly concentrated), that the responsiveness of equilibrium quality to the rise in the size of the market accessible to producers is greatest. Thus, it is in those industries where the high pre-globalization level of concentration is re-established via a shakeout process, that the greatest global welfare gains are generated in Phase III.

Box 5.2. Ace Designers: Knightian Uncertainty and Capability Building

We already met the Ace Designers company in Section 4.7, where we looked at the founders' success in establishing themselves as India's leading seller of CNC lathes. Ace Designers' success was based on building the type of basic CNC lathe that was most popular in the Indian market in the 1990s: a 'single spindle, two axis' machine. By 2000, Ace had decided to concentrate its product development efforts on the design of a more sophisticated type of machine – one for which there would not, in the near future, be a market in India large enough to allow the firm to recoup its investment. The thinking behind this strategy was one of 'investing in capability'. Ace's owners knew that, over the next couple of decades, as India's economy grew, real wage rates for skilled machinists would rise to the point where a more sophisticated type of machine would be favoured: just as had happened in the advanced industrial economies.[3]

But this would all be far in the future. For Ace, its present R&D project would not be directly justifiable on the basis of likely profits from its next generation of machines. Rather, the firm was looking to a longer horizon. Without advancing its capabilities to multi-spindle, multi-axis machines, it would lack the sophistication that would be needed to compete with foreign competitors who would serve the Indian market in the next generation.

How should we think of this 'investment in capability building' from an analytical point of view? In Sections 1.5 and 5.2, we look at investment in capability building in the conventional way, i.e. we suppose the firms have a given cost function $F(u_i)$ and know their payoff function $\pi(u_i; \{u_{-i}\})$. But in the case of a firm faced with Ace's predicament, it is hard to maintain this classical economic assumption that all firms have access to a payoff function (whether a deterministic one of the kind we use here, or one containing a standard stochastic element). Such a notion presupposes that there are some possible future 'states of the world' to which Ace can attach (at least subjective) probabilities. But Ace Designers could not do this, any more than we as outside observers; even to list the possible states of the world. In India's machine tool market a generation hence is too difficult.

Investments in capability building by firms quite often have this flavour: the decision to build capability is one that is taken, not on the basis of some explicit estimation of likely costs and benefits, but rather on the basis of a much more intangible judgement as to the pluses and minuses of going in a given direction. The natural way to analyse such a decision would be to cast in the setting of 'Knightian Uncertainty' – i.e. a setting in which we eschew any attempt to combine an exhaustive listing of future scenarios, with a probability attached to each. This kind of analysis is difficult, and the literature has grappled with models of this kind, on and off, for fifty years: but there is no settled view in the profession as to the best way to design and analyse models of this kind.[4]

---

[3] The more sophisticated ('multi-spindle, multi-axis') machines carry out several operations on a job before the machined piece is released. This economizes on skilled manpower, while raising the cost of capital: a classic switch to a more capital-intensive method of production as labour costs rise.

[4] For an interesting and radical viewpoint on such issues, see Kay (2011).

5.3. INTO THE WINDOW?

In this section, we turn to the bottom end of the window, and to the fortunes of Sub-Saharan African firms that now face the challenge of 'getting into the window' and entering global manufacturing.

During the 1990s, as India and China forged ahead, it seemed to many observers that the countries of Sub-Saharan African were being left behind. This impression was underlined by the relatively low share of Foreign Direct Investment that flowed to the region. Why were FDI flows so low? We already saw one part of the answer in Chapters 3 and 4. For industries where 'absorbtive capacity' matters, India, China, and Eastern Europe were more attractive targets for FDI, since they offered equally low wages while having a more developed industrial base. (This was illustrated in Figure 3.4, where the country at point X dominates all countries of lower income: the poorer countries offer no advantage in terms of wage rates, and their manufacturing capabilities are at a lower level.[5] See also Chapter 4, Box 4.2.)

So what are the manufacturing capabilities of Sub-Saharan African countries?

In addressing this question, it is useful to return to the perspective of Chapter 2, where we examined the cross-country relationship between capabilities and wealth. One sharp warning that emerged from our empirical explorations in Chapter 2 was that the range of countries active in the production and export of products from any conventionally classified industry is liable to be extremely wide – and so it is treacherous to look for any tight classification of industries associated with any band of national wealth. With that cautionary lesson in mind, I will here confine myself to a single, admittedly very crude, distinction between two groups of manufacturing industries. To motivate the distinction I am about to introduce, I want to backtrack a little and ask: what industries do we typically find in the larger Sub-Saharan countries?

To make things concrete, consider the cases of Ethiopia, Ghana, and Tanzania, for each of which a full and detailed survey of industrial capabilities is now available.[6]

---

[5] For a fuller and more nuanced analysis of the pattern of FDI flows in this period, see Crafts and Venables (2005).

[6] Sutton and Kellow (2010), Sutton and Kpenty (2012), Sutton and Olomi (2012). These volumes can be downloaded free of charge from http://personal.lse.ac.uk/sutton/.

Among the industries that are well established and fairly highly developed are Food and Drink, Cement, and Building Materials. In contrast to this, the Metals, Engineering, and Assembly sector is at a low level of development, as is the Plastics sector. What is the crucial difference? Firms in the Food and Drink, Cement, and Building Materials industries can survive and prosper while serving the local market. A certain degree of 'natural protection' is afforded by transport costs (cement) and perishability (some food products). More importantly, these are *final* products, that are sold direct to consumers. Imported products do compete with local products, often fiercely. But there are many local producers who have levels of quality and productivity that are often good and sometimes very good by international standards, and have built up a strong and long-established market position, that can (or could) be sustained with low (or zero) tariff protection.

But the Metals, Engineering, and Assembly sector, and the Plastics sector, are different. What kinds of activity do we typically find in these sectors? Local steel production from domestically sourced scrap is common, but the range of steel products produced locally is very restricted. Basic products such as drawn wire and corrugated sheet are widely produced by highly capable (often mid-size) firms. So too are basic plastics products, such as pipes, cables, and domestic utensils.

But the core products of the global industry are absent. What distinguishes the core products that are traded internationally is that they are predominantly *intermediate* goods that are sold from one firm to another. They enter into the production of final goods whose many components will be sourced from a (possibly quite large) number of different firms in a well-developed and complex international supply chain. And in this setting, the demands on firms are higher. The sophistication of manufacturing processes required to meet the quality demands of global final goods producers is of a higher order than is required for local success in Food and Drinks, or Cement, or Building Materials. We've already seen an example of this in the auto-component sector in Chapter 3, where we looked at the way in which Indian and Chinese companies brought themselves 'into the window' over the decade beginning in the mid-1990s. Indeed, one of the most striking features of industrial development in China and India over the past two decades is the way in which firms made this transition. Crossing this hurdle now forms the key challenge for the industries of Sub-Saharan Africa.

A caveat is in order here. New Zealand is a rich country with a relatively low proportion of manufacturing exports entering international supply chains. Its wealth derives to an important degree from its success as an agricultural exporter. Norway, too, has a low proportion of such exports; one key contributor to its wealth is its exports of oil and gas. So high-level manufacturing capabilities are indeed a road to riches, in the words of Peter Jay (2001). But they are not the only road, and if a country is fortunate enough to enjoy extensive natural resources, and has the social and political institutions that allow these to be exploited efficiently for the benefit of all, then it can prosper without advanced manufacturing exports.

And yet: no theme is more prevalent right now in the area of African economic development than the drive to industrialize. And, Africa's natural resource base notwithstanding, it is hard to see how the new-found hopes for Africa's economic progress can be realized for most of the region's economies without a step change in the level of industrial capabilities.

The hope is everywhere. A decade ago, there was little but gloom. The liberalization of the early 1990s had benefitted some of the poorer countries, but an overly rapid opening up of local industries in some of the more prosperous countries in the region (and especially in Zambia) led to the wiping out of key domestic industries. But much has changed in the past decade. In line with what we saw in the model of Chapter 3, globalization has swung the terms of trade in favour of metals and oil exporters, and so in favour of many countries in Sub-Saharan Africa. This has contributed to rates of growth in several of the larger Sub-Saharan economies since 2000 that are dramatically higher than those in the leading industrial economies. And this in turn has led to a new optimism. For the first time in a generation, there is a sense that a group of major economies in Sub-Saharan Africa can make the transition into full participation in the new global supply chains that now dominate the world's manufacturing activity.

The lessons from India and China suggest this will not happen without a serious upsurge in Foreign Direct Investment, which alone provides a general pathway towards advancing industrial capabilities in type (ii) sectors. No imperative is more important to current policy than the crafting of measures that will enhance this process. The circumstances vary widely from one country to another in the region. For Ghana, with its new-found oil wealth, the challenge is to forge a bridge between its oil sector and its domestic Metals, Engineering, and

Assembly sector Sutton and Kpenty (2012). For Ethiopia, the challenge lies in creating channels that can better facilitate the entry of a large number of mid-size companies across the manufacturing spectrum (Sutton and Kellow, 2010). The details vary, but the underlying challenge is the same. The next decade will mark a crucial turning point in Africa's economic development; and the shaping of policy measures that push forward the process of capability building, rather than hold it back, will be central to the continent's future.

APPENDIX 1.1

Solving the Model

Deriving equations (1.5) and (1.6). I will ease notation in what follows by suppressing the subscript from w_i, w_j. (All firms face the same wage.)

The profit of firm i is:

$$\Pi_i = p_i x_i - w c_i x_i \tag{1.1.1}$$

$$= \lambda u_i x_i - w c_i x_i$$

where

$$\lambda = \frac{S}{\sum_j u_j x_j} \tag{1.1.2}$$

It is useful to express the first-order condition in terms of λ. Note that:

$$\frac{\partial \lambda}{\partial x_i} = -\frac{S}{\left(\sum_j u_j x_j \right)^2} \frac{\partial \sum_j u_j x_j}{\partial x_i}$$

$$= -\frac{S u_i}{\left(\sum_j u_j x_j \right)^2}$$

$$= -\frac{u_i}{S} \lambda^2 \tag{1.1.3}$$

The first-order condition for profit maximization is:

$$\frac{\partial \Pi_i}{\partial x_i} = \lambda u_i + \frac{\partial \lambda}{\partial x_i} u_i x_i - w c_i = 0 \tag{1.1.4}$$

On substituting for $\frac{\partial \lambda}{\partial x_i}$, from (1.1.2) and (1.1.3), and rearranging, this becomes

$$u_i x_i = S \left(\frac{1}{\lambda} - \frac{w c_i}{\lambda^2 u_i} \right) \tag{1.1.5}$$

Summing over j, we have,

$$\sum_j u_j x_j = S\left(\frac{n}{\lambda} - \frac{1}{\lambda^2}\sum_j \frac{wc_j}{u_j}\right) \tag{1.1.6}$$

where the sum is taken over all firms (products) for which $x_j > 0$, and n denotes the total number of such firms.

From (1.1.2) we have $\sum_j x_j u_j = \dfrac{S}{\lambda}$ so that

$$\frac{S}{\lambda} = S\left(\frac{n}{\lambda} - \frac{1}{\lambda^2}\sum_j \frac{wc_j}{u_j}\right)$$

whence

$$\lambda = \frac{1}{n-1}\sum_j \frac{wc_j}{u_j} \tag{1.1.7}$$

Substituting this expression for λ in (1.1.5), we have on rearranging that

$$x_i = \frac{S(n-1)}{u_i \sum_j \dfrac{wc_j}{u_j}}\left(1 - \frac{n-1}{\dfrac{u_i}{wc_i}\sum_j \dfrac{wc_j}{u_j}}\right) \tag{1.1.8}$$

which, on rearranging, and writing wc_j/u_j as k_j, yields equation (1.5) of the text. We can solve for prices using $p_i = \lambda u_i$, whence from (1.1.7) we have

$$p_i - wc_i = \left(\frac{1}{n-1}\frac{u_i}{wc_i}\sum_j \frac{wc_j}{u_j} - 1\right) wc_i \tag{1.1.9}$$

Inserting (1.1.8) and (1.1.9) into the profit function and simplifying, we obtain

$$\Pi_i = S\left(1 - \frac{n-1}{\dfrac{u_i}{wc_i}\sum_j \dfrac{wc_j}{u_j}}\right)^2 = \left[1 - (n-1)\frac{k_i}{\displaystyle\sum_{j\ st\ x_j>0} k_j}\right]^2 S$$

which is equation (1.6) of the text.

Properties of the Output Function

Proof of Part 1. Using equation (1.5), note that $\sum_j k_j = \sum_j \dfrac{w_j c_j}{u_j}$ is increasing in w_i, and $\dfrac{k_i}{\sum_j k_j} = \dfrac{w_i c_i / u_i}{\sum \frac{w_j c_j}{u_j}}$ is increasing in w_i, whence the r.h.s. expression in (1.5) falls.

Proof of Part 2. From equation (1.5) it follows on rearranging that

$$x_i = \frac{S}{w_i c_i}(n-1)\frac{w_i c_i / u_i}{\displaystyle\sum_j \frac{w_j c_j}{u_j}}\left\{1 - (n-1)\frac{w_i c_i / u_i}{\displaystyle\sum_j \frac{w_j c_j}{u_j}}\right\}.$$

We aim to examine how x_i varies with u_i, holding w_i, c_i and the w_j, c_j and u_j constant, over the relevant domain (where the inequality is satisfied, to be defined precisely below).

With this in mind, define the function

$$z(u_i) = \frac{w_i c_i / u_i}{\displaystyle\sum_j \frac{w_j c_j}{u_j}} = \frac{1}{1 + \dfrac{u_i}{w_i c_i}\left(\displaystyle\sum_{j \neq i} \frac{w_j c_j}{u_j}\right)}$$

and note that $z(u_i)$ is strictly decreasing. Note that

$$x_i = \frac{S}{w_i c_i}(n-1) \times z[1 - (n-1)z]$$

The relevant domain can be written in terms of z as

$$\frac{1}{n} < z \leq \frac{1}{n-1}$$

where the right-hand inequality corresponds to the threshold at which u_i reaches the level at which firm i's effective cost level $w_i c_i / u_i$ makes the firm just viable, while the left-hand inequality corresponds to the point at which firm i's effective cost level $w_i c_i / u_i$ becomes equal to that of its $n-1$ identical rivals, so that $z(u_i) = 1/[1 + (n-1)] = 1/n$.

To establish that x_i is increasing in u_i on the relevant domain, we note that the function $z[1 - (n - 1)z]$ is strictly decreasing on the domain

$$\frac{1}{2}\frac{1}{n-1} < z \leq \frac{1}{n-1}.$$

Recall that $n \geq 2$, whence this domain includes the relevant domain

$$\frac{1}{n} < z \leq \frac{1}{n-1}.$$

It follows that $\partial x_i / \partial u_i > 0$ on the relevant domain.

Proof of Part 3. Consider equation (1.5). Since u_i/w_i and hence $w_i c_i/u_i$ are constant, the r.h.s. of equation (1.5) is constant. Hence, so is $x_i u_i$. Since u_i is rising, it must be that x_i is falling.

The Viability Threshold

We saw in the text that if there are n_0 firms, indexed by j, each of which is strictly viable (i.e. $x_j > 0$ for all j), then the critical threshold of effective cost below which a potential entrant becomes viable is given by

$$\frac{1}{n_0 - 1} \sum_{j=1}^{n_0} k_j \tag{1.3.1}$$

We now ask the question: how does the entry of new firms affect this threshold? It is intuitively clear that the entry of a new firm that is strictly viable will lower the threshold. It is also intuitively clear that the entry of a new firm that is strictly non-viable (in the sense that its value of k is strictly above the threshold level given by (1.3.1)) will not have any effect on the level of this threshold. This raises an obvious question: what happens if we introduce a new firm whose capability level coincides exactly with (1.3.1)? This firm is exactly on the threshold of viability: it has an output of zero, so we should expect intuitively that it does not affect the viability threshold (1.3.1). This is indeed the case, as the following calculation shows:

Denote, as before, the total number of firms initially in the market as n_0, and suppose that all these firms are strictly viable. Consider a new firm, labelled firm l, which is on the threshold of viability specified by (1.3.1), i.e.

$$k_l = \frac{1}{n_0 - 1} \sum_{j=1}^{n_0} k_j \tag{1.3.2}$$

Now suppose firm l enters the market. This implies that the number of firms has risen from n_0 to $n_0 + 1$, and the sum $\sum_{j=1}^{n_0} k_j$ is now replaced by $\sum_{j=1}^{n_0+1} k_j$, so that the viability threshold (1.3.1) is now replaced by

$$\frac{1}{n_0} \sum_{j=1}^{n_0+1} k_j$$

$$= \frac{1}{n_0} \left(\sum_{j=1}^{n_0} k_j + k_l \right)$$

$$= \frac{1}{n_0}\left(1 + \frac{1}{n_0 - 1}\right)\sum_{j=1}^{n_0} k_j$$

$$= \frac{1}{n_0 - 1}\sum_{j=1}^{n_0} k_j$$

which coincides with (1.3.1).

Two remarks are in order:

(i) This result justifies the use of the strict inequality in the sum taken in defining the viability condition (1.7) of the text, i.e. we can define the condition by counting the number of firms with $x_j > 0$.

(ii) If we also include additionally some firm(s) on the threshold of viability, then this makes no difference: we obtain the same value for the threshold.

Re-deriving the 'Level of Activity' Equation

An alternative way of deriving and interpreting equation (1.25) is as follows.

We have taken all fixed costs as being sunk, and treated the number of firms n, and the capabilities of firms, measured by u and c, as given. It follows that in this constant returns setting, as the population rises, all that happens is that S rises in direct proportion to N. We can therefore think of the way things work by considering each individual in the economy choosing individual labour supply

$$l^S = \frac{n-1}{n} \frac{u}{c} \qquad (1.4.1)$$

and consuming

$$\left(\frac{n-1}{n}\right)^2 \frac{u}{c} \frac{1}{c}$$

units of the good, thereby achieving utility

$$U = \frac{1}{2} \left(\frac{n-1}{n}\right)^2 \left(\frac{u}{c}\right)^2$$

The economy comprises N workers, each making this decision.

Now consider the level of gross national expenditure, denoted by S. From the individual labour supply schedule (1.4.1), the total wage bill in the economy is

$$Nwl^S = Nw \frac{n-1}{n} \frac{u}{c}.$$

The markup $\frac{p}{wc}$ equals $\frac{n}{n-1}$, so total national income (including the income of non-workers) is

$$\frac{n}{n-1} \times Nw \frac{n-1}{n} \frac{u}{c} = Nw \frac{u}{c}$$

which equals S by definition.

Hence, as before, we have

$$\frac{1}{w} \cdot \frac{S}{N} = \frac{u}{c}.$$

APPENDIX 2.1

Perfect Sorting

The set of goods G_k produced by the firms in country k comprise the m goods in product group k, all of whose producers face the same country-specific wage rate, which we denote by w_k, and have the same level of output (for each of the m products in product group k). We denote the equilibrium level of output of each product g by the single firm in each producing country k as x_{gk}. It follows from the basic output equation of Chapter 1 that, if all active producers have the same productivity and quality levels, then, setting $c = 1$ to ease notation,

$$x_{gk} = \frac{n_g - 1}{n_g^2} \frac{S}{w_k} \tag{2.1.1}$$

so the total demand for labour in a country of type k is

$$L_k^D = \sum_{g \in G_k} x_{gk} = \sum_{g \in G_k} \frac{n_g - 1}{n_g^2} \frac{S}{w_k} = m \frac{n_k - 1}{n_k^2} \frac{S}{w_k} \tag{2.1.2}$$

where the sum over $g \in G_k$ comprises the m products in G_k, and where n_k denotes the (common) value of the number n_g of producers of any good $g \in G_k$, which in the present special case equals the number of countries of type k, or n_k.

We now turn to labour supply: it follows from the form of equation (2.1) and the fact that there are N workers in each country that the labour supply function for country k takes the form of a ray through the origin, namely

$$L_k^S = w_k N \prod_g \left(\delta \frac{u_g}{p_g} \right)^\delta \tag{2.1.3}$$

where w_k is the wage rate in country k and where δ corresponds, as before, to the share of expenditure devoted to good g (which we have assumed to be equal for all goods).

Since equations (2.1.1) and (2.1.2) already incorporate product market equilibrium, we may characterize general equilibrium by equating the supply and demand for labour within each country (type).

Labour market equilibrium requires, given the form of the labour supply function (2.1.3), that for any two country types k and k',

$$\frac{L_k^S}{L_{k'}^S} = \frac{w_k}{w_{k'}} = \frac{L_k^D}{L_{k'}^D}$$

whence on substituting in equation (2.1.2) for any two country types k and k' we have

$$\frac{w_k}{w_{k'}} = \sqrt{\frac{n_k - 1}{n_{k'} - 1} \cdot \frac{n_{k'}}{n_k}} \tag{2.1.4}$$

This equation serves to define the chain of wage ratios between country type k' and country type k.

Up to this point, we have assumed that firms from country group k are the sole producers of product group k. We now note that the restriction on the n_k introduced above, namely $n_k \geq n_{k+1} + 4$, ensures this is so. To do this, note that a necessary and sufficient condition for this is that firms in each country $k + i$ have wages $w_{k+i} > w_k$ sufficiently high to render them unviable in the production of good k. Using the basic viability condition of Chapter 1 with the inequality reversed and recalling that u denotes the common standard of quality shared by all active firms in the market, this requires that

$$\frac{w_{k+i}}{w_k} > \frac{n_k}{n_k - 1}$$

From equation (2.1.4), a sufficient condition for this is that, for all k,

$$\frac{w_{k+1}}{w_k} = \sqrt{\frac{n_{k+1} - 1}{n_k - 1} \frac{n_k}{n_{k+1}}} > \frac{n_k}{n_k - 1} \tag{2.1.5}$$

It is easy to verify that, given our assumption that $n_k \geq 2$ for all k, this inequality follows from our assumption that $n_k \geq n_{k+1} + 4$ for all k. In terms of our earlier discussion, this quantifies the degree to which the higher ranked good $k + 1$ requires a scarcer capability than good k.

This establishes that under our restrictions on the n_ks there will be perfect sorting in equilibrium. That is, there will be a $1 : 1$ mapping between country types and product groups.

The Export Basket

As explained in the text, for each product g, Sutton and Trefler (2012) identify the poorest and richest exporters of the product. (Data on exports is easy to assemble consistently across countries, while data on productivity is not.) Denote these by $y_{min,g}$ and $y_{max,g}$, respectively, where g indexes the good (or industry) in question. It is important to avoid 'noise' associated with small reported export values, a problem to which trade data are notoriously prone. To do this, we identify the set of countries for whom the good is a 'significant' export, in the sense that the value of its export in that good constitutes at least 1 per cent of the value of exports of the country's principal export good. (The exact value used for the cut-off is arbitrary, but changing it to $\frac{1}{2}$ per cent or 2 per cent does not materially affect the results.)

The data used is the standard data for international data statistics, and is at the usual level of aggregation, denoted SITC 4.

The striking feature that emerges from this analysis is that the income range between the poorest and the richest country, i.e. the range from $y_{min,g}$ to $y_{max,g}$, is very wide for the majority of SITC 4 industries. (Moving to lower levels of aggregation does not ease this problem, moreover.)

There are two distinct groups of industries that have a relatively narrow range. The first group consists of those goods exported only by relatively low-income countries (the 'L group'). The second group consists of those goods exported only by relatively high-income countries (the 'H group'). On our present interpretation, L-group goods are not produced by high-income countries because these countries' wage costs are too high, whereas H-group goods are not produced by low-income countries because their quality capabilities are too low.

It is interesting to focus on the relationship between a country's GDP per capita with (a) the share of L goods in its exported basket and (b) the share of H goods in its export basket. Sutton and Trefler (2012) note that while countries exporting a high proportion of H goods are always rich, it is not the case that rich countries are necessarily significant exporters of H goods. Similarly, while a high share of L goods necessarily implies that a country is poor, many poor countries have a low share of L goods.

We can interpret this as follows: The middle group of wide-range goods, or 'M-goods', incorporates a set of products, or qualities of a product, that require levels of capability ranging from very low, to very high. In other words, we are dealing with inherent limitations of this kind of data.

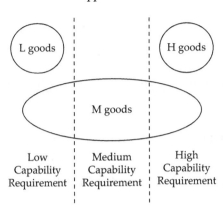

Fig. A2.2.1. Capability Requirements versus ISIC Industry Definitions

If we map goods in terms of their 'true' requirements in terms of capabilities, we would get the kind of pattern shown in Figure A2.2.1. Some of those goods that require a high level of manufacturing capability will be *H* goods, others will be classified among the *M* goods. Likewise, some of the goods requiring only a low level of manufacturing capability will be *L* goods, while some will be classified among *M* goods. And so:

- a country that exports mostly *L* goods is a low-income country. But a low-income country doesn't necessarily make only *L* goods (it may make low-quality *M* goods);
- a country that exports mostly *H* goods is a high-income country. But a high-income country doesn't necessarily export mostly *H* goods (it may mostly export high-end *M* goods).

In other words, in looking for a link between a country's export basket and its wealth, using conventional trade statistics, it is important to bear in mind that wide-range *M* goods are the norm, and the data carries only limited information on underlying manufacturing capabilities.

The Welfare Indicator for Country C

The utility indicator for Country C is

$$U_C = \frac{1}{2}\left(\frac{w_C}{M}\right)^2 \prod_{i=1}^{M}\left(\frac{u_i}{p_i}\right)^{2/M} \qquad (4.1.1)$$

where

$$\frac{p_u}{u} = \frac{p_v}{v} = \frac{n}{2n-1}\left[\frac{w_A + w_C\mu}{u} + \frac{w_B + w_C\mu}{v}\right] \qquad (4.1.2)$$

and $w_C = \mu(w_A + w_B)$. Writing w_B/w_A as ω, we have

$$w_C = \mu w_A(1+\omega),$$

whence

$$w_A = \frac{1}{1+\omega}\cdot\frac{w_C}{\mu} \quad \text{and} \quad w_B = \frac{\omega}{1+\omega}\cdot\frac{w_C}{\mu} \qquad (4.1.3)$$

so that

$$\frac{p_u}{u} = \frac{p_v}{v} = \frac{n}{2n-1}\frac{w_C}{\mu}$$

$$\cdot\left\{\left[\frac{1}{1+\omega}(1+\mu^2)+\mu^2\frac{\omega}{1+\omega}\right]\frac{1}{u} + \left[\frac{1}{1+\omega}\mu^2 + \frac{\omega}{1+\omega}(1+\mu^2)\right]\frac{1}{v}\right\}$$

$$= \frac{n}{2n-1}w_C\left\{\mu\left(\frac{1}{u}+\frac{1}{v}\right)+\frac{1}{\mu}\left(\frac{1}{1+\omega}\cdot\frac{1}{u}+\frac{\omega}{1+\omega}\cdot\frac{1}{v}\right)\right\} \qquad (4.1.4)$$

Substituting in (4.1.1) we have

$$U_C(v;u) = \frac{1}{2M^2}\left(\frac{2n-1}{n}\right)^2 \frac{1}{\left\{\mu\left(\frac{1}{u}+\frac{1}{v}\right)+\frac{1}{\mu}\left(\frac{1}{1+\omega}\cdot\frac{1}{u}+\frac{\omega}{1+\omega}\cdot\frac{1}{v}\right)\right\}^2}$$

When $v = u$, whence $\omega = 1$, this reduces to

$$U_C(u;u) = \frac{1}{2M^2}\left(\frac{2n-1}{n}\right)^2\frac{u^2}{\left\{\frac{1+2\mu^2}{\mu}\right\}^2} \qquad (4.1.5)$$

On the other hand, when $v = v^c = \frac{n-1}{n} \cdot \frac{1}{1+1/\mu^2} \cdot u$, whence $\omega = 0$, it reduces to

$$U_C(0; u) = \frac{1}{2M^2} \left(\frac{n-1}{n} \right)^2 \frac{u^2}{\left\{ \frac{1+\mu^2}{\mu} \right\}^2} \qquad (4.1.6)$$

If follows that

$$\frac{U_C(u; u)}{U_C(0; u)} = \left[\frac{2n-1}{n-1} \cdot \frac{1+\mu^2}{1+2\mu^2} \right]^2$$

which is greater than 1 on the relevant domain $n \geq 2$, $\mu \geq 0$.

Bibliography

Amiti, M. and A. Khandelwal (2009): 'Import Competition and Quality Upgrading,' *NBER Working Paper*.

Aslund, A. (1994): 'Lessons of the First Four Years of Systemic Change in Eastern Europe,' *Journal of Comparative Economics*, 19(1), 22–38.

Atkeson, A. and P. Kehoe (2005): 'Modeling and Measuring Organization Capital,' *Journal of Political Economy*, 113(5), 1026–53.

Balassa, B. (1967): 'Trade Creation and Trade Diversion in the European Common Market,' *The Economic Journal*, 77(305), 1–21.

Baldwin, R. and J. Harrigan (2011): 'Zeros, Quality, and Space: Trade Theory and Trade Evidence,' *American Economic Journal: Microeconomics*, 3(2), 60–88.

Bastos, P. and J. Silva (2010): 'The Quality of a Firm's Exports: Where you Export to Matters,' *Journal of International Economics*, 82(2), 99–111.

Bernard, A., J. Jensen, and P. Schott (2006): 'Survival of the Best Fit: Exposure to Low-Wage Countries and the (Uneven) Growth of US Manufacturing Plants,' *Journal of International Economics*, 68(1), 219–37.

Bernard, A., S. Redding, and P. Schott (2010): 'Multiple-Product Firms and Product Switching,' *American Economic Review*, 100(1), 70–97.

Bernard, A., S. Redding, and P. Schott (2011): 'Multiproduct Firms and Trade Liberalization,' *The Quarterly Journal of Economics*, 126(3), 1271–318.

Bloom, N. and J. Van Reenen (2007): 'Measuring and Explaining Management Practices Across Firms and Countries,' *Quarterly Journal of Economics*, 122(4), 1351–408.

Brandt, L., T. Rawski, and J. Sutton (2008): 'Industrial Organization,' *China's Great Economic Transformation*, Cambridge: CUP.

Choi, Y., D. Hummels, and C. Xiang (2009): 'Explaining Import Quality: The Role of Income Distribution,' *Journal of International Economics*, 77(3), 265–75.

Clark, K. and T. Fujimoto (1991): *Product Development Performance: Strategy, Organization, and Management in the World Auto Industry*. Harvard Business Press.

Cohen, W. and D. Levinthal (1990): 'Absorptive Capacity: A New Perspective on Learning and Innovation,' *Administrative Science Quarterly*, 35(1), 128–52.

Crafts, N. and A. Venables (2005): 'Globalization in History: a Geographical Perspective,' in *Globalization in Historical Perspective*, ed. by M. Bordo, A. Taylor, and J. Williamson. University of Chicago Press.

Feenstra, R. (1984): 'Voluntary Export Restraint in U.S. Autos, 1980–1981: Quality, Employment, and Welfare Effects', in *The Structure and Evolution of Recent U.S. Trade Policy*, ed. by R. Baldwin and A. Krueger. University of Chicago Press.

Fujita, M., P. Krugman, and A. Venables (1999): *The Spatial Economy: Cities, Regions and International Trade*. MIT Press.

Garicano, L. and T. Hubbard (2005): 'Hierarchical Sorting and Learning Costs: Theory and Evidence from the Law', *Journal of Economic Behavior & Organization*, 58(2), 349–69.

Garicano, L. and T. Hubbard (2007): 'Managerial Leverage is Limited by the Extent of the Market: Hierarchies, Specialization, and the Utilization of Lawyers' Human Capital', *Journal of Law and Economics*, 50(1), 1–43.

Garicano, L. and T. Hubbard (2009): 'Specialization, Firms, and Markets: The Division of Labor within and between Law Firms', *Journal of Law, Economics, and Organization*, 25(2), 339–71.

Gibbons, R. and R. Henderson (2011): 'Relational Contracts and Organizational Capabilities', *Organization Science, Article in Advance*, pp. 1–15.

Goldberg, P. and N. Pavcnik (2007): 'Distributional Effects of Globalization in Developing Countries', *Journal of Economic Literature*, 45(1), 39–82.

Gomulka, S. (1991): 'The Causes of Recession Following Stabilization', *Comparative Economic Studies*, 33(2), 71–90.

Grossman, G. and E. Helpman (1991): *Innovation and Growth in the Global Economy*. MIT Press.

Grubel, H. and P. Lloyd (1975): *Intra-industry Trade: the Theory and Measurement of International Trade in Differentiated Products*. Macmillan.

Hallak, J. (2006): 'Product Quality and the Direction of Trade', *Journal of International Economics*, 68(1), 238–65.

Hallak, J. and P. Schott (2011): 'Estimating Cross-Country Differences in Product Quality', *Quarterly Journal of Economics* 126(1), 417–74.

Hallak, J. and J. Sivadasan (2009): 'Firms' Exporting Behavior under Quality Constraints', *NBER Working Paper*.

Hausmann, R. J. Hwang, and D. Rodrik (2007): 'What You Export Matters', *Journal of Economic Growth*, 12(1), 1–25.

Hortaçsu, A. and C. Syverson (2007): 'Cementing Relationships: Vertical Integration, Foreclosure, Productivity, and Prices', *Journal of Political Economy*, 115(2), 250–301.

Hummels, D. and P. Klenow (2005): 'The Variety and Quality of a Nation's Exports', *The American Economic Review*, 95(3), 704–23.

Hummels, D. and A. Skiba (2004): 'Shipping the Good Apples Out? An Empirical Confirmation of the Alchian–Allen Conjecture', *Journal of Political Economy*, 112(6), 1384–402.

Javorcik, B. (2004): 'Does Foreign Direct Investment Increase the Productivity of Domestic Firms? In Search of Spillovers through Backward Linkages', *The American Economic Review*, 94(3), 605–27.

Jay, P. (2001): *Road to Riches or The Wealth of Man*. Phoenix.

Johnson, R. (2012): 'Trade and Prices with Heterogeneous Firms,' *Journal of International Economics*, 86(1), 43–56.

Kay, J. (2011): *Obliquity: Why Our Goals are Best Achieved Indirectly*. Profile Books.

Khandelwal, A. (2010): 'The Long and Short (of) Quality Ladders,' *Review of Economic Studies*, 77(4), 1450–76.

Kiguel, M. and N. Liviatan (1992): 'The Business Cycle Associated with Exchange-Rate-Based Stabilizations,' *The World Bank Economic Review*, 6(2), 279–305.

Kornai, J. (1993): 'Transformational Recession: A General Phenomenon Examined through the Example of Hungary's Development,' *Économie Appliqué*, 46(2), 181–227.

Krugman, P. (1979): 'Increasing Returns, Monopolistic Competition, and International Trade,' *Journal of International Economics*, 9(4), 469–79.

Krugman, P. (1997): *Pop Internationalism*. MIT Press.

Kugler, M. and E. Verhoogen (2012): 'Prices, Plant Size, and Product Quality', *Review of Economic Studies*, 79(1), 307–39.

Lall, S., J. Weiss, and J. Zhang (2006): 'The 'Sophistication' of Exports: A New Trade Measure,' *World Development*, 34(2), 222–37.

Lockett, A., S. Thompson, and U. Morgenstern (2009): 'The Development of the Resource-based View of the Firm: A Critical Appraisal,' *International Journal of Management Reviews*, 11(1), 9–28.

Michaely, M. (1984): *Trade, Income Levels, and Dependence*, Studies in International Economics. North-Holland.

Mostafa, R. and S. Klepper (2011): 'Industrial Development through Tacit Knowledge Seeding: Evidence from the Bangladesh Garment Industry,' *Unpublished Working Paper*.

O'Rourke, K. and J. Williamson (2001): *Globalization and History: the Evolution of a Nineteenth-Century Atlantic Economy*. MIT Press.

Penrose, E. (1959): *The Theory of the Growth of the Firm*. New York: John Wiley.

Prescott, E. and M. Visscher (1980): 'Organization Capital,' *The Journal of Political Economy*, 88(3), 446–61.

Roland, G. and T. Verdier (1999): 'Transition and the Output Fall,' *Economics of Transition*, 7(1), 1–28.

Rumelt, R. (1984): 'Towards a Strategic Theory of the Firm,' in *Competitive Strategic Management*, ed. by R. Lamb, pp. 556–70. Englewood Cliffs, NJ: Prentice Hall.

Schott, P. (2004): 'Across-Product Versus Within-Product Specialization in International Trade,' *Quarterly Journal of Economics*, 119(2), 647–78.

Schott, P. (2008): 'The Relative Sophistication of Chinese Exports,' *Economic Policy*, 23(53), 5–49.

Shaked, A. and J. Sutton (1983): 'Natural Oligopolies,' *Econometrica*, 51(5), 1469–83.

Stokey, N. (1991): 'Human Capital, Product Quality, and Growth,' *The Quarterly Journal of Economics*, 106(2), 587–616.

Sutton, J. (1991): *Sunk Costs and Market Structure: Price Competition, Advertising, and the Evolution of Concentration.* MIT Press.

Sutton, J. (1998): *Technology and Market Structure: Theory and History.* MIT Press.

Sutton, J. (2001): 'Rich Trades, Scarce Capabilities: Industrial Development Revisited,' in *Proceedings of the British Academy*, vol. 111, pp. 245–74. Oxford University Press.

Sutton, J. (2004): 'The Auto-component Supply Chain in China and India – A Benchmark Study,' *World Bank*.

Sutton, J. (2007a): 'Market Structure: Theory and Evidence,' *Handbook of Industrial Organization*, 3, 2301–68.

Sutton, J. (2007b): 'Quality, Trade and the Moving Window: The Globalisation Process,' *The Economic Journal*, 117(524), F469–F498.

Sutton, J. and N. Kellow (2010): *An Enterprise Map of Ethiopia.* International Growth Centre.

Sutton, J. and B. Kpenty (2012): *An Enterprise Map of Ghana.* International Growth Centre.

Sutton, J. and D. Olomi (2012): *An Enterprise Map of Tanzania.* International Growth Centre.

Sutton, J. and D. Trefler (2012): 'Capabilities, Wealth and Trade,' *NBER Working Paper*.

Symeonidis, G. (2002): *The Effects of Competition: Cartel Policy and the Evolution of Strategy and Structure in British Industry.* MIT Press.

Syverson, C. (2008): 'Markets: Ready-Mixed Concrete,' *The Journal of Economic Perspectives*, 22(1), 217–34.

Verhoogen, E. (2008): 'Trade, Quality Upgrading, and Wage Inequality in the Mexican Manufacturing Sector,' *Quarterly Journal of Economics*, 123(2), 489–530.

Von Hippel, E. (1994): ' "Sticky Information" and the Locus of Problem Solving: Implications for Innovation,' *Management Science*, 40(4), 429–39.

Wernerfelt, B. (1984): 'A Resource-based View of the Firm,' *Strategic Management Journal*, 5(2), 171–80.

Winiecki, J. (1991): 'The Inevitability of a Fall in Output in the Early Stages of Transition to the Market: Theoretical Underpinnings,' *Soviet Studies*, 43(4), 669–76.

Womack, J., D. Jones, and D. Roos (1990): *The Machine that Changed the World*, Free Press Paperbacks. Rawson Associates.

Young, A. (1991): 'Learning by Doing and the Dynamic Effects of International Trade,' *The Quarterly Journal of Economics*, 106(2), 369–405.

Author Index

Subject Index

Printed in the USA/Agawam, MA
March 17, 2023

807146.001